# UNRESOLVED LIVES

SEVEN STORIES OF MAYHEM INCLUDING THE MAD BUTCHER, SODDER CHILDREN, AND CABIN 13

BY SUSAN WILLIAMS

# UNRESOLVED LIVES

### SEVEN STORIES OF MAYHEM INCLUDING THE MAD BUTCHER, SODDER CHILDREN, AND CABIN 13

BY SUSAN WILLIAMS

Charleston, WV

Charleston, WV

Copyright 2024 Susan Williams

All rights reserved. No part of this book may be reproduced in any form or means, electronic or mechanical, including photocopying, recording, or by any information storage and retrieval system, without permission in writing from the publisher.

ISBN-13  978-1-942294-73-3

Back cover photo: John Williams

*Distributed by:*

**West Virginia Book Company**
1125 Central Ave. Charleston, WV 25302
www.wvbookco.com

## Table of Contents

Introduction ............................................................................. vi

Chapter 1: The Sodder Fire ................................................... 1

Chapter 2: The Mad Butcher ................................................ 14

Chapter 3: A Surreal Interview with the Mad Butcher ......... 28

Chapter 4: Donald and Theresa Woods ................................ 33

Chapter 5: Cathy Carroll ....................................................... 38

Chapter 6: Eddie Brown ........................................................ 70

Chapter 7: Rev. Michael Flippo ............................................ 76

Chapter 8: The Great Unknown ........................................... 98

# Introduction

Murder casts a shadow over families. Once a loved one is lost to murder, the ensuing shadow covers most aspects of life. The dishes washed, the showers taken, the shifts worked might seem like examples of a normal life. But the shadow overtakes everything, blocking out any hoped for light.

In the worst cases, the loved one disappears. These family members never see an end to their grief. They never get to draw a line under any chain of events. They grapple with this stupendous mystery. How can someone just disappear?

Moving down the ladder one rung, families who never see someone held accountable for the murder rank next in suffering. These people bear their grief and rage daily without the cover of resolution. They can roll endlessly over the known events that filled the last minutes and hours of the life lost. "Endlessly" is the key word.

Even for families lucky enough to see a murderer convicted, there are always memories that spring to life unexpectedly with the glance of an old picture or the sound of a favorite song. They live in dread of dates on the calendar.

Their lives hang in suspension like pieces in amber. Their growth is stunted emotionally. Just as we might stretch our arms as far as we can to enjoy movement itself, they can only stretch their lives and spirits so far before they bump into those barriers murder imposed on their unresolved lives.

They wait for the day their hearts do not ache. They wait for the morning they will awake without a thought of pain and loss.

In Fayette County, I grew up seeing the billboard with the sad faces of the Sodder children staring down at us. I also grew up in the shadow of fear created by the Mad Butcher.

As a reporter for *The Charleston Gazette*, I wrote about these two cases many times, and I introduced myself to the surviving family members in the other cases included here.

## Vanished

On Christmas Eve 1945, George and Jennie Sodder took their youngest child to their bedroom and let their other children stay up to play with their new toys. A few hours later when their house caught on fire, George and his older sons fought the blaze. As the ashes cooled, the parents began a new phase of their lives, searching and wondering what happened to five of their children that they never saw again. *This story is in Chapter 1.*

On Oct. 20, 1962, after he worked his shift at the Four Minute Lunch in Oak Hill, Sammy Smith either walked or hitchhiked to another nearby restaurant, the Top Hat Drive-In. He drank a cup of coffee and said goodnight to everyone around him. He was a short distance from his family home where his mother waited for him. He was never seen again. All these decades later, his body has not been found. But his name was added to the list of likely victims of the man who earned the name the Mad Butcher.

As readers, we find it hard to wrap our heads around the fact that people can disappear. One moment they are with us —the next they have vanished. Imagine how difficult the disappearance is for their families. *This story is in Chapter 2.*

## Grief consumes health

Besides the obvious loads of grief they carry, many family members sink into depression and early death. This constant pain of loss aggravates health problems.

Donald Woods knew as soon as he received the phone call telling him his daughter did not return home after school that something was seriously wrong. He sometimes called the 13-year-old a scaredy cat. He started searching for her immediately.

In a painful irony, Woods took posters of his missing daughter to Montgomery City Hall. He met Cathy Roberts Carroll, a city employee, who promised him she would distribute some of the posters. But soon in a completely different case, Cathy was tortured and murdered.

Woods told me how he suffered, not knowing where his daughter might be. The uncertainty only ended when her remains were found. *This story is in Chapter 4.*

In their shared grief and frustration, Donald Woods became friends with Edward Roberts, Cathy's father. The two men knew the depth of despair they could feel. Both fathers and Mrs. Roberts died early, their grief likely figuring into their deaths. To this day, no one has been arrested for the murder of either daughter. *This story is in Chapter 5.*

## Why no arrest?

An examination of the facts would argue an arrest should have been made years ago for Eddie Brown's killer. Brown, always kind and generous, was attacked on his way to work. But no one has claimed the reward offered for information leading to an arrest. *This story is in Chapter 6.*

## Conviction

The Right Rev. Michael Flippo was beloved by his church families, and he and his devoted wife had three healthy sons they were raising in a series of parsonages. But Flippo always wanted bigger houses, bigger churches, a bigger income. He cooked the books at several of his churches and fundraisers. He torched several churches, too. He burned at least two parsonages where his children barely escaped the flames. He was never charged with embezzlement or arson. But once his wife was beaten to death, a close examination of Flippo's life produced an unsettling picture.

He was convicted of his wife's murder and is serving a prison sentence. But his wife's siblings continue to suffer the loss of someone they describe as so kind and caring. His sons lost their mother to violence and then lost their father to his incarceration. *This story is in Chapter 7.*

## The great unknown

I know almost nothing about this man except for the fact no one missed him. In *Hamlet*, the prince wonders if it is better "to be or not to be." What if a person is not even acknowledged in life or death? This traveler to "the undiscovered country" arrived early and alone. He died nameless. *This is the last Chapter, number 8.*

I deem it a privilege that family members who lost their loved ones let me share some of their time. We hoped that if I wrote something about their cases some answers might emerge. I wish I could have done more, and once again I am sharing these stories.

To write these stories, I interviewed all the surviving family members I could find. Several of them talked to me many times in hopes of keeping their loved ones alive in the public eye.

With the cases in this book that produced indictments, I read each court file. I have my own copy of former Fayette County Sheriff Bill Laird's 281-page investigative report into the Carroll case. Because accuracy is so important to me, I think I read it about a half dozen times.

With the Rev. Flippo, I covered each appeal he filed with both the West Virginia Supreme Court of Appeals and the United States Supreme Court.

I covered each court hearing that related to all of the cases.

Police and prosecutors were generous to me with their time.

# Chapter 1
# The Sodder Fire

*The death or disappearance of five children is a heartbreaking tragedy. I cannot imagine facing the death of one child. To confront the loss of five children all at once is more than most of us could endure. But for George and Jennie Sodder the loss of five of their 10 children was a tragedy they had to face every day of their lives. To ask people not to forget their children, the Sodders built an iconic billboard near their home that featured pictures of the children. Fundamental questions about what happened to their children have never been answered to this day. A strong case can be made that the Sodders were victims of people bent on revenge. More than 75 years after it started, this fire is still debated.*

No one who saw the billboard forgot it.

The faces of five children stared sadly down from a specially made billboard outside of Fayetteville on West Virginia 16. The faces seemed to ask drivers to help them find their way home.

The billboard was erected after a fire broke out in the home of George and Jennie Sodder on Christmas Eve 1945. The Sodders were the parents of 10 children.

After the fire, five of their children were never found. Although a par-

# The Sodder Fire

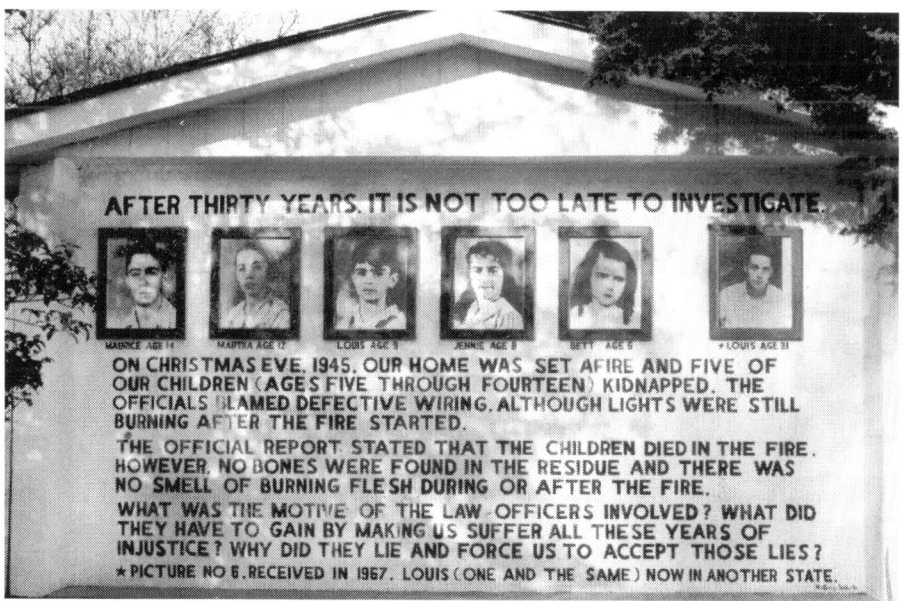

The iconic billboard of the five missing Sodder children.

tially burned dictionary was discovered in the ashes of the fire, no bones or evidence of the children's bodies ever surfaced.

I am a retired *Charleston Gazette* reporter, and I have written about this case several times. I am not a forensic expert, but I firmly believe the children did not die in the fire.

The distraught parents spent the rest of their lives and thousands of dollars trying to find their children. The case gained national exposure at the time at the time and still does. It even attracts international attention.

Police, private investigators, and crackpots filled up a thick case file with information. Now Internet sleuths try their hands with the case, too.

My friends Melody and George Bragg researched and wrote about the case for their book, *West Virginia Unsolved Murders*. Melody told me that before she started, she assumed the Sodders could not accept their children's deaths. Who could? But by the time she completed her work, Melody, too, came away with more questions than answers.

On Christmas Eve 1945, all the Sodders were at home except their son Joe, who was still in the Army. With World War II coming to an end, he was expected home soon. The family lived in a large two-story home with a full basement.

Sodder made his living working on trucks and had some engines in the basement. He also had an office on the first floor equipped with a telephone.

The children opened their presents on Christmas Eve and were in no hurry to go to bed. Mr. and Mrs. Sodder let them stay up, retired to their bedroom on the first floor, and took their youngest daughter with them.

At 12:30 a.m., Mrs. Sodder was awakened when the phone rang. She answered the phone, but it was a wrong number. The Sodders heated their home with coal stoves, so she checked them while she was up, and then went back to bed.

She was awakened about a half hour later by the sound of something — maybe a rock — being thrown on the roof. She went back to sleep again. Next, she awakened from the smell of smoke.

She got her husband up and yelled for the two oldest boys, John and George Jr., who were asleep upstairs.

The two older sons believed the younger children were on their way downstairs. Outside, Sodder and his two sons tried to fight the fire.

They soon realized the younger children were not coming down the stairs. Sodder would later tell police that a ladder was always leaning against the house. But that night, the ladder was gone.

When he could not find the ladder, Sodder wanted to start a truck and back it up to the house, climb onto the cab, and try to reach the children. The first truck he tried would not start. The second truck was dead, too.

While her father and brothers fought the fire, daughter Marion ran to a neighbor's house to call the Fayetteville Fire Department. But they could not reach the telephone operator. Another neighbor passing by also called but could not reach an operator either.

The fire department did not arrive until 8 a.m. Christmas Day, many hours after the fire broke out.

The family could not find 14-year-old Maurice; 12-year-old Martha Lee; 9-year-old Louis; 8-year-old Jennie and 5-year-old Betty. It is their faces that stared down at drivers on W.Va. 16 for years.

After the fire department watered down the smoldering embers, people began to rake through the ashes looking for the children's remains. No remains were ever found.

When I interviewed him, Jim Roles was 85 and the only surviving member of the Fayetteville Fire Department who was on call that day. "We looked through ashes all day. I don't think they (the children) burned up in there," he told me.

Roles said they never smelled burning flesh. No one else at the fire ever reported smelling burning flesh or heard any sound from the children.

Dazed and grief stricken, four days later, the Sodders had the ground bulldozed and flowers planted.

But later questions started to crop up that no one could answer. A telephone repairman told them lines to their home had been cut — not burned. People who gathered to watch the fire reported seeing someone steal a block and tackle from the garage.

After the fire, Mr. Sodder, who like his wife, was born in Italy, began to recall a threat made to him by another Italian American who lived in Fayetteville. The man, now dead, allegedly said, "Your goddam house is going to go up in smoke and your children are going to be destroyed."

The man also raged against Sodder for criticism Sodder made of Mussolini.

Sodder had been a partner with this man and he would benefit from a clause in the Sodders' mortgage. The man ended up on the coroner's jury that declared the fire an accident.

Sodder's former partner had co-signed a note for the Sodders payable to the Bank of Fayetteville. Sodder had $1,500 insurance on his house with a mortgage clause payable to the same man.

The Fayetteville fire chief that responded to the fire was also the bookkeeper for the same man.

The fire chief, the late J.F. Morris, did not arrive at the fire until 8 a.m. Later, when the fire was investigated, Morris admitted he received two telephone calls asking him to come to the fire. When the caller alerted Morris that the Sodder home was burning, Morris admitted and replied, "We know about it."

Morris said he could not drive the fire truck, so he had to wait until he could find someone to drive it. Morris is also responsible for a bizarre twist to the case. A police report states, "Morris cannot or will not offer any explanation for his peculiar and apparently secret handing of (liver)."

For reasons known only to him, Morris buried what turned out to be a beef liver in a box in the ashes. The liver was dug up two years after the fire. The family had a mortician examine it that certified it was a beef liver and had never been exposed to fire.

Morris' actions came to light after he told a minister at the Fayetteville Baptist Church that he had found a heart in the ashes. Morris also told the minister that hearts do not burn. Of course, this is not true. Some later reports attribute the quote to the minister.

When the family heard about Morris' remark, they asked him to come to the home and help them find what he had buried. They had to call him several times before he finally came. He helped them to find the box with the liver in it that he had buried.

Several police and fire marshal reports criticize Morris for this still unexplainable action. Bob Lane Bragg has a fuller explanation of this terrible step Morris took in his book, *No Direct Evidence: The Story of the Missing Sodder Children.*

As they sought answers, the Sodders received a report from The Cincinnati Cremation Company. A staff member explained they burn bodies for two hours at 2,000 degrees, but, even then, some bones remain intact.

Fayetteville funeral home director C.J. Dodd also wrote in 1951 he could not believe the children were in the fire. Dodd and his son happened to be driving by at the time the house was on fire and stopped. Later he wrote, "In view of the fact and considering the short length of time the house burned, it is my opinion that the Sodder children did not perish in the fire."

In Texas, two years after the fire, reporters wrote about a chain of events that began with one ship in the port of Texas City. The French-registered ship, the *SS Grandcamp*, exploded April 16, 1947. *Wikipedia* combined newspaper accounts from the time that explained the ship had about 2,300 tons of ammonium nitrate in its cargo. The ship was also carrying small arms ammunition, machinery, cotton, peanuts, tobacco, and twine.

The longshoremen who loaded the ammonium nitrate that was packaged in paper sacks reported the bags were warm to the touch.

Around 8 a.m., smoke was visible from the ship, and the captain thought perhaps if he sealed all hatches, the fire could be smothered. But the ammonium nitrate exploded. The blast from it produced a 15-foot shockwave that leveled nearly 1,000 buildings on land.

Flying shrapnel ignited refineries and chemical tanks along the waterfront. Two sightseeing planes were blown out of the sky. Half the widows in Galveston were shattered. The explosion blew almost 6,350 short tons of the ship's steel into the air, some at supersonic speed.

Another ship, the *High Flyer*, also exploded as a consequence, and some witnesses thought the second ship's explosion was even more powerful than the first.

Of course, the Sodder house fire was in no way comparable to the series of events that happened in Texas with chain reactions fed by so many explosives and fuel. But people who have studied both events noted that even with such force, bodies were recovered in Texas.

Of the dead in Texas, 405 were recognizable. In some cases, it took days to recover the bodies from the ships. But as experts noted, the bodies were still recognizable as human.

In 1951, Assistant Fire Marshall C.R. Cobb wrote in a report, "It is impossible to determine the cause of the fire. No motive or evidence of arson has been found and no outstanding hazard is known that might have resulted in an accidental fire."

To this day, the cause of the fire has not been determined. Some people speculated that it was electrical. But Mrs. Sodder said in early interviews that she was told, if it were electrical, the lights would have gone out. She distinctly remembered the lights were on when she discovered the fire. When the family was outside, she also remembered seeing their Christmas lights go out.

Believing the children must have been kidnapped, the Sodders hired several private investigators to try to help them find the children. They turned to police and politicians, asking for help, but they never got anywhere. The FBI even got involved, but they closed the case in 1952.

In one report, a Fayette County Prosecutor stated he did not want to open a case against people he had to work and eat with.

The private investigators did not produce any results, but they drained a great deal of money from the family.

In 1949, Sodder hired a pathologist from the Smithsonian in Washington, D.C. This was after a search of the grounds turned up four lumbar vertebrae. The pathologist concluded the bones had never been exposed to fire. The Sodders came to believe that the four vertebrae arrived in the fill dirt, possibly from a cemetery in Mount Hope, when they filled in the basement and laid wreaths for their children's graves four days after the fire.

In the report from the Smithsonian, Marshall T. Newman wrote, "Since the house was stated to have burned only for a half hour or so, one would expect to find the full skeletons of the five children."

The Sodders had many reports that their children were sited in different places around the United States. One rumor even claimed the children were kidnapped and in a taxi watching as their home burned.

A Smithers woman allegedly told someone the children were brought to her home after the fire. Then someone with Florida license plates took the children away. This story was investigated but came to nothing.

Police and the FBI investigated stories that the children were in Florida. Even a Cortes County Commissioner claimed that he had seen them.

The family also offered a reward. Someone who signed his letter, "a miner who needs money," offered information still in the police file, but it lead nowhere.

Someone even tried to tie the mysterious disappearances of the children to another case that also attracted national attention. In the 1960s, people in Fayette County were terrorized by the man they dubbed the Mad Butcher. But there are no connections between the two cases.

Mr. Sodder traveled to a school in New York after he saw a picture of a child in the school who looked like one of his children. He was not allowed in the school to see the child, though.

In 1968, the Sodders received a photo through the mail of a young man in his 20s. The name "Louis Sodder" was written on the back. That is the last picture added to the famous billboard.

If the children were alive, no one ever contacted the Sodders with ransom demands.

In one police report, someone noted that private investigators bled the Sodders "for the sole purpose of confusing the Sodder family and extorting every cent they earn."

The case was traumatic for the Sodder children who survived the fire. Sylvia Sodder Paxton was the toddler who slept in her parents' room the night of the fire.

She remembered watching the house burn from inside her father's truck. His arm was bleeding after he broke out a window, while trying to rescue his other children.

Over the years, she remembered how her father paced the floors, wondering about his children. He died in 1969. Her mother moved into Paxton's St. Albans home for the last years of her life and died in 1989. The children agreed to sell the family home. They took down the famous billboard before new owners came along.

As evidence, Mrs. Sodder kept pieces of linoleum and catalogues that survived the fire. To her, they were confirmation that the children could not have perished in the fire, Paxton said.

As the youngest, Paxton spent more time with her parents than the older children did. She remembered the anguish they suffered.

Her older brother John, told me of their parents, "They left this world disappointed because they never knew what happened."

Sylvia Sodder Paxton wanted to carry on the search for her brothers and sisters on behalf of her parents. "I would love to know what happened. I know they could not have been there in the fire. It's like you come to the end of a story, and there's no end," Paxton said.

## Sodder fire revisited

Hosted by Laurence Fishburne, *History's Greatest Mysteries* devoted an episode to the Sodder Fire. If there could be a chance any of the questions that hang over this case could be answered, I was glad to see this subject taken up.

The experts who assembled to discuss this case agreed, they didn't think the children died in the fire.

I also think that the Sodder family was punished for speaking out against a dangerous oaf. Remember, Benito Mussolini was Hitler's partner as they slaughtered their way around Europe and North Africa in World War II. Mussolini was another power-hungry leader who was large on visions of grandeur and small on brains.

Mr. and Mrs. Sodder were both born in Italy. Two of their American born sons joined the fight during World War II against Mussolini and Hitler. How tragic to see the Sodder family suffer because misguided people thought Mussolini should not be criticized.

Hate fueled the fire and incompetence kept it from ever being solved.

In the *History's Greatest Mysteries* episode, one theorist speculated that the children ran away. I reject this as completely without merit. The last thing the children did was play with new Christmas gifts. Considering their ages, I cannot imagine that they would turn from playing and think: let's run away on a cold Christmas Eve night. There is no evidence to support this theory.

Once the fire broke out and people gathered around the house, men were seen around the house and one man was seen clearly stealing a block and tackle.

As Mr. Sodder said, he always had a ladder against his house. But on the night of the fire, it was missing.

After they started the fire, I believe the kidnappers used the ladder to reach the children on the second floor. The children smelled smoke. The kidnappers told the children: your house is on fire. We are here to rescue you. So, the children gladly followed them down the ladder.

After the fire, a telephone repairman told the Sodders their lines had been cut, not burned. The Sodders got no help from local authorities to follow up on the evidence from the night of the fire.

The hardest question to answer in this case is why did the children never contact their family, and I have no answer for that. It is difficult to understand why simple curiosity would not compel at least one child to return home.

Immediately after the fire, I think the children were told that all of their family died in the fire. I am sure they were told: you are the only survivors. You are lucky I saved you. That would halt the children's questions at first. Considering the limited communications at the time, the children would believe whatever their captors told them.

More than 30 years ago, I bought a home in Falls View Village. I learned soon after I moved in that Ted and Elsie Sodder were my neighbors. Their home was surrounded by tall, chain link fencing, the only house in the village with this kind of fencing.

Like his father, George "Ted" Sodder, Jr. had his own business. He was president of Sodder Trucking Company in Alloy, a few miles from his home. I only ever saw him wearing work clothes. Elsie worked at Montgomery General Hospital. Her dark hair was always perfect. Everyone who ever saw Elsie would agree that she was always neatly dressed. She favored white blouses.

I learned from another neighbor that Elsie always wanted children, but Ted was too traumatized by his early life and would not agree. Elsie clearly loved Ted and was absolutely devoted to his care until the end. When his health deteriorated and he had to be on oxygen, she installed all the equipment he needed, including a generator when the power went off. She slept on the floor by his bed so that she would be ready instantly for any help he might need.

In 2021, he died at home at age 83.

Ted and Elsie paid educational expenses for some of their nieces and nephews and always treated their nieces and nephews to vacations and special events.

When the 50th anniversary of the fire approached, I asked Elsie if I could interview her and Ted for the story I would write for *The Charleston Gazette*. She politely declined, and I always respected her feelings on the subject. I never asked a second time.

When we came to their home, Elsie always invited us in, and we would sit in the kitchen and enjoy a good talk. She was famous for her cooking, and would not let us leave without taking food. She would always tell us she was glad we came for our annual Christmas visit.

Although Ted was older than Elsie, they both lived to be 83.

## Last known child

Years after I first interviewed her, Sylvia Sodder Paxton died in 2021. When I read her obituary, I was glad to know she had a happy life. She enjoyed true love in her marriage and healthy children and grandchildren. She fed her family with the Italian food her mother taught her to make and "country cooking" she learned from her mother-in-law.

But even against the background of this happy life, Sylvia never forgot all of her brothers and sisters. She was the youngest Sodder child, and lived to be 79. In her obituary, she listed her four older siblings who survived the fire and who died before her. But she also listed the names of her five siblings who were never seen after the fire.

This moved me so much. Even at her death, she wanted to put their names out for everyone to remember one more time.

The mystery of the Sodder fire survives her.

## Chapter 2
## **The Mad Butcher**

*Before 1962 in West Virginia, most police officers would say that the few murder cases they investigated had roots in anger, jealousy, or theft. But after police found a young man's body cut-up into 13 pieces, police and the public alike had to face an entirely different and completely unheard of kind of murder. The brutality of the murder shocked everyone. Its senselessness was also startling. As police realized men were disappearing, they began to talk of the Mad Butcher.*

As night began to fall in Fayette County in the early 1960s, few children waited for their mothers to call them home. A vague uneasiness and visions conjured up from overhearing pieces of adult conversations sent them home willingly. They knew that somewhere, out there in the dark, the Mad Butcher waited.

As 1962 drew to its end, county residents were shocked and horrified by a hideous crime. Someone — perhaps even a neighbor — was responsible for an atrocity never before known in their towns.

On Dec. 27, 1962, a young boy looking for pop bottles and hubcaps on Gauley Mountain found a body. A dismembered body. It lay in 13 pieces scattered over the mountainside.

His discovery marked the beginning of police investigations that even-

*Unresolved Lives*

tually included seven victims.

Although dozens of other unsolved murders have been committed in Fayette County since then, none shook residents' security so thoroughly or attracted more national attention than the crimes of the Mad Butcher. Detective magazine writers cranked out stories about it. More recently, the late writer Breece D'J Pancake of Milton used the material for his short story, "Time and Again."

Now, decades later, new state troopers assigned to the Oak Hill detachment still try their luck with the thick, tattered files that grew out of the investigation. Each trooper hopes to bring a fresh perspective to the case, and perhaps, finally solve it.

Retired Trooper G.L. Swartz, who was the first officer to work on the case full-time, said, "We never got close to an arrest. We eliminated some suspects. Some suspects were never eliminated." Eventually, suspicious disappearances stopped, and no more bodies were found.

Because the bodies were so meticulously dismembered, many police officers believed a doctor, or a professional meat cutter was responsible. A former sheriff's brother-in-law was a suspect. He was a meat cutter who eventually moved

Mike Rogers was only 18 when police found his body cut-up in 13 pieces that were flung over Gauley Mountain. His remains were found Dec. 27, 1962. Although Rogers' body was the first found, as police investigated, they discovered he was not the first victim of the man who would become known as the Mad Butcher. *Courtesy GEM Publications*

out of state. This suspect had a walk-in meat cooler at his grocery store, Swartz said. Mike Rogers, the victim found cut in 13 pieces, often hung around there, Swartz said. Another suspect committed suicide.

Two doctors who worked in the Oak Hill area were considered suspects.

A chief suspect was a member of two prominent Fayette County families, and both families had political connections.

The suspect imagined he was a doctor. Police said he had been assigned to a pathology unit in the military and attended a year of pre-medicine classes at West Virginia University. Sources speculated the man believed he was operating on his victims.

He was eventually arrested in November 1964 for destruction of property when he took a sledgehammer to the Laird Memorial Hospital in Montgomery. He had been refused a job there as a doctor. Former Smithers Police Chief E.S. Goodson arrested the suspect after he fled to Smithers.

Goodson said the man had a small meat grinder, a child's toy stethoscope, guns, and a knife in his car when he was arrested. Goodson said he also recovered a gun from the man's apartment, but it could not be positively identified as the gun that killed Rogers before he had been dismembered.

Goodson took fingerprints of Mike Rogers' corpse at the funeral home. He said the joints were surgically cut and left no doubt in his mind they were made by someone with medical training.

The suspect was quietly institutionalized.

Trooper Swartz tried to question him after he was taken to the mental hospital in Spencer. "The doctor promised me faithfully he'd get in touch with me. But when I arrived, the patient was gone, the doctor was gone, and the records were gone. That was negligence on the doctor's part."

Trooper Swartz said, "I thought there were some attempts to stall my visit by hospital personnel. My superiors just told me that's the way it goes."

Swartz said he was not encouraged to pursue the suspect with a court order.

In time, the man was transferred to a mental hospital in Dayton, Ohio, but he also maintained a private residence in Dayton. Contacted by phone, the suspect told me he had been out of the hospital for long periods of time and had been questioned about other brutal murders outside West Virginia. He said he was allowed to leave the hospital on the first and third Tuesdays of each month and could be released from the hospital again.

The hospital superintendent refused to confirm his statements. She said such privileges are a part of a patient's treatment and cannot be discussed.

In 1962, Trooper Swartz identified the first victim as Mike Rogers, a teenager with mental deficiencies. He was often seen listening to a transistor radio on Oak Hill streets. The murderer stuffed Rogers' remains into a duffle bag and threw it over Gauley Mountain, scattering its contents down the hillside.

"It was a terrible case," Trooper Swartz said. "It kind of got to me. I was having nightmares — working on it day and night. Mike's body had been hung like a carcass of beef — feet first. The blood was drained out of it. It was cut in joints like you would butcher an animal."

The duffle bag was the only physical evidence Swartz had other than the body. Swartz traced the ownership of the bag, but the original owner lost the bag years earlier when he changed buses in Gauley Bridge.

Friction between the sheriff's department and state police worked against a solution. State police officers had caught several deputies running numbers (a way of gambling). "They resented it," Trooper Swartz said. "It was so bad that I would go in to interview someone and find out a deputy had been there ahead of me and told them not to talk to me."

G. L. Swartz was transferred to McDowell County after a year. He never worked full time on the case again.

\*\*\*

Shirley Gene Arthur was handsome and talented, his sister said. The 33-year-old man had just begun a promising singing career. He sang country songs and recorded some gospel music.

As a Navy man, he was decorated for saving a life and was also a member of the crew to pick up the first astronaut who splashed down. Personal problems made him leave the Navy without permission and come home.

Although Geneva Gilland did not know it at the time, her brother died on the same day as John F. Kennedy. On Nov. 22, 1963, Arthur had dinner with his parents in Bradley, West Virginia. His father drove him to his girlfriend's home, and he planned to hitchhike back to his parents' house. He ate a yellow apple and freshly made coconut cake at his girlfriend's home.

"He never ate again," his sister said. "The last meal we know he had was still in his stomach." The coroner's report said an autopsy found a yellow apple and coconut among the stomach contents.

Some men found a torso Dec. 7, 1963, near Pineville. Although some authorities disagreed, Gilland is confident it was her brother. The stomach contents matched what she knew he ate, but his Navy dog tags did not match the blood type of the torso. Several people who investigated the case believe the dog tags could have been wrong, or the torso's blood might have been incorrectly typed.

"The FBI said it wasn't him. They wouldn't even let us have it. They buried it in a wooden box near Pineville," Gilland said. Her brother had a tattoo and dental records that could have positively identified him, but his head and arms were never found. A coroner's jury later ruled the torso was Arthur's.

Gilliand's brother was stabbed 19 times in the heart. The autopsy said he must have been naked because there were no clothing fibers in the heart. He probably was already dead because there were no jagged edges to the wounds to indicate a struggle. The lower part of the torso was wrapped in burlap, and there was straw in the burlap.

"This destroyed my family," Gilland said. "My father died of a heart attack at 59, a few months after my brother was found. He grieved himself to death. My mother had a stroke. Used to be I could not talk about it. I loved my brother so much."

During her father's funeral, FBI agents waited in the back of the church, Gilland said. If Arthur was alive and came to his father's funeral, the FBI would have arrested him for being AWOL.

"My other brother, who sang with Shirley, just quit singing. He couldn't do it anymore," Gilland said.

Seven years after the torso was discovered, Gilland had her brother declared legally dead. "I had to do it for his little boy, so he could get a check."

Geneva's mother would never accept that the youngest of her nine children was dead. "She'd wake up screaming, 'Go find my baby!' My father would go out and search the road where he'd been hitchhiking."

All through the years, Geneva Gilland said she has tortured herself wondering, "Did he suffer? Did he have a chance to pray?"

"The state police in Beckley finally told us they closed the case. It was just wasting their time, they said."

"It's been such a long time people think you're supposed to forget. When this first happened, I couldn't even smile. I felt guilty if I smiled. It's just as real today as it was then. It never leaves you. If we could have buried him, we could have gotten over it better. It's not just the one who died. It's the whole family," Geneva said.

\*\*\*

Sammy Smith, 33, had been working on a Connecticut tobacco farm. After he returned to his parents' home in Scarbro, he got a job washing dishes at the Four Minute Lunch on Main Street in Oak Hill. He did not have a car.

After work Oct. 20, 1962, he either hitchhiked or was offered a ride south to the Top Hat Drive-In. He drank a cup of coffee and said good night to everyone there about 12:15 a.m, his brother Louis said witnesses told him later. He was never seen again. Police added his name to those who disappeared during the reign of the Mad Butcher.

Sammy Smith's mother, Eva, was 84 when I interviewed her. Although her son had been missing for 26 years at that time, she still kept his room spotlessly clean.

Sammy Smith, 33, worked as a dishwasher at the Four Minute Lunch on Main Street in Oak Hill.
*Courtesy GEM Publications*

She remembered, "He got up Saturday morning and I shampooed his hair and fixed his breakfast. That was the last time I ever saw him."

Louis Smith said his brother was liked by everyone. "He would take time to talk to people. He was good and kind."

Mrs. Smith's home is filled with pictures of her family. Near the chair where she was sitting when I interviewed her was a striking picture of her as a young woman. She shuffled through dozens of photographs she took of her son working in the garden or dressed for church.

She said she dreamed one night her son came to her and stood by her bed. In her dream, she asked him, "Sammy, how did you get away from here?" He told her, "I went with three boys."

"To me, it's like he's not dead. But having a missing child, that's worse on you than following a loved one to the graveyard. If I hadn't been serving the Lord, I would have been crazy by now," Mrs. Smith said.

\*\*\*

Three other men disappeared between the roughly two-year period from February 1962 to December 1963. They have never been heard from and their bodies never found. The course of their lives, though, shares some common ground with the other victims. Whether those similarities and coincidences are by accident or design may never be known.

One of the three victims who was never found was U.S. Army Sgt. James Lee Haynes. He was hitchhiking from Baltimore to his parents' home in Maben in Wyoming County.

Later a Powellton woman who saw Haynes' picture in the newspaper told police she picked up a soldier who looked like the newspaper photograph. She said the man talked to her about his wife and children in Baltimore. She drove him to Main Street in Oak Hill, where she let him out at 2:30 p.m. Dec. 7, 1963, the same day Shirley Gene Arthur's torso was found.

Haynes' body was never found. He was a career soldier and not AWOL. A letter in state police files dated Jan. 15, 1965 indicated he was still missing.

A frequent hitchhiker, Mack Agee, 29, of Kingston, West Virginia, disappeared after he visited his mother in an Oak Hill nursing home in February 1962. Some confusion among family members over who was to report him missing may account for why police did not have a missing person's report for him until July 4, 1964. In the files police accumulated on this case, information about Agee makes up the thinnest file.

Ernest Esker Gwinn, 76, was a retired railroad worker who rented a room from the owners of the Four Minute Lunch. He disappeared around the Fourth of July 1962, before Rogers' body was found cut-up in 13 pieces. Once Rogers was found, police suspected foul play in Gwinn's disappearance. Gwinn's son Nick, who was 74 when I interviewed him, said, "I still hope someday I might find out something."

A seventh man, Lou Bennett, was last seen at the Four Minute Lunch

July 27, 1963. Bennett, 42, was a mine operator. After his wife reported him missing, police added his name to their list.

Bennett's body was later found outside of Oak Hill Sept. 29, 1965. But police do not think he was a victim of the Mad Butcher.

\*\*\*

J. Zane Summerfield went on to become a Fayette County Circuit Judge before he retired. But he was the county prosecutor when the first body was found. He told me he narrowed his list of suspects to two people.

Summerfield sent a skull and some leg bones to the Smithsonian Institution for analysis. Some railroad workers found the bones near Claremont, a former coal mining community. The bones were determined to be a man's bones, but the analysts could not say with certainty that they belonged to any of the missing men.

Police were also stumped by the butcher's methods. Mike Roger's dismembered body was the only complete body found. Rogers was large, weighing more than 200 pounds. Police said it would have taken a long time to dismember his body, but they could never find a place, like a barn, where this might have happened. The straw found in the burlap around Arthur's torso also seemed to indicate a barn could have been used.

Trooper Swartz said, "It's hard to believe one person did it. It was weird." He also said he could never decide on a motive for killing Mike Rogers. "He was harmless. It could have been someone who was sick. Or it could have had sexual overtones."

Mike Rogers was often seen in front of the Four Minute Lunch. Ernest Gwinn was a customer and also rented a room from the restaurant's owners. Sammy Smith worked there. Lou Bennett was last seen there.

Questions about what role the restaurant could have played in the murders and disappearances still abound.

A man who spoke Spanish married a woman who lived near the victim Mike Rogers. The man quarreled with his wife and accused her of infidelities. In 1967, he separated from his wife and moved to Michigan where he began to work on a farm. He wrote a letter in Spanish that accused his wife of using Rogers as a go-between for her lover. In his letter, the aggrieved husband wrote that the lovers met at the Four Minute Lunch.

After he completed the letter, he shot himself. The people who found his body could not read Spanish. They turned the letter over to the police who at first thought it must be the depressed man's thoughts as he said goodbye to life. Months later, after the letter was translated, Michigan police contacted West Virginia police after they realized the information in the letter might help solve the Mad Butcher case. But the allegations of an adulterous affair had nothing to do with the murders.

How many of these men would still be alive if they had not hitchhiked or accepted rides from someone they thought they knew? Arthur, Haynes, and Agee were each hitchhiking. Smith, Rogers, and Gwinn did not have cars.

In his own mind, Trooper G. L. Swartz never singled out one of the suspects as the killer. "I learned in this kind of work that you should never decide this is it. So many things can go wrong. I kept an open mind."

Even after he transferred out of Fayette County and later retired from police work, Swartz said, "I still keep my eyes open on that case. I always hoped that someone would solve it."

## A prime suspect

Although Trooper G. L. Swartz may have kept an open mind, my late friend George Bragg and I have always been convinced we knew who the Mad Butcher was. Bragg and his wife Melody wrote about the Mad Butcher in their book, *West Virginia Unsolved Murders*.

Independently, George and I each talked to our prime suspect by phone. George made a tape of his telephone call, and he included a transcript of the call in their book. I still have my handwritten notes.

The suspect was never charged with murder. I started my newspaper career at a small newspaper, but even when I went to *The Charleston Gazette*, I was always cautious about being sued.

George gave the suspect the name "Simon Chapple" in their book. From George's research, he was convinced that the prime suspect committed butcher murders in other states, including Oklahoma and Texas. The suspect lived in both of these states.

George had a strong sense of right and wrong that I always admired. He pursued several murderers for interviews that always made me fearful that he could get hurt.

While he worked on the case, Trooper Swartz discovered that the suspect's family whisked the man out of Spencer State Hospital before Swartz could arrive to question him.

I knew the suspect was related to two families with political connections. The suspect was never charged with murder. If he had been, every writer could use that public document and his name.

George and I, and mutual friends who knew the suspect, believed we had the right person. But what if we were wrong? We could harm the suspect as well as his family. In many instances, naming the wrong person could also harm the case, but this case has never been solved. So, I chose not to use the name of the person I believe was responsible for the murders.

## Escapes

Once his family moved him to a mental health facility in Ohio, the suspect lived in Dayton until he died in 1997 at age 79.

But he did not always stay in the facility. He left it on several occasions. In 1985, he was found in St. Albans, where he had a friend.

In 1991 close to Halloween, the suspect walked away from the Dayton Mental Health Center. Fayette County Sheriff Bill Laird was in office at the time, and officials notified him. Laird's family founded Laird Memorial Hospital in Montgomery. The only time the suspect was ever arrested was for destruction of property after he took a sledgehammer to the hospital. People speculated the suspect might try to return to Montgomery where he still has relatives.

Ohio hospital officials would only say that a then 63-year-old man walked away from the facility Oct. 25. The suspect was 6 feet-four inches tall and weighed 210 pounds.

## New technologies

In 1962, Mike Rogers' body was found on Gauley Mountain and so was the duffle bag that held his remains. Rogers was the only complete body found during the investigation of this case.

Obviously, in 1962, researchers were limited in what they could do with fiber and blood evidence. The duffle bag was housed in the Oak Hill detachment of the State Police.

It should still be there, safe, and ready to be of use should anyone know how to explore it with advanced technology.

It is not there. I was extremely frustrated when I learned it had been allowed to leave the evidence room. A former Fayette County deputy told a trooper that he thought he knew someone who might recognize the bag.

The deputy, who is now dead, never returned the bag. I have no patience for this kind of incompetence. The bag held many secrets, and modern technology might have been able to draw them out of the darkness.

The families who have waited for so long for any answers might have had at least a few with modern technology. In all aspects of life, accountability is crucial. Crimes cannot be solved without accountability to procedures.

## Why?

When I interviewed the man I believe to be the Mad Butcher, he explained that people are either sacrifices or executioners. He thought he had to kill or be killed.

That might have been his justification, but it still does not explain the butchery. He wanted to be a doctor, and he had some training in the medical field. He was also in love with a doctor's daughter.

Of course, my thoughts are pure speculation, but I think that he wanted to see how the human body ticked. If he cut open a specimen, he could see how the systems of the body were fitted and worked together.

He told me the Holy Spirit came over him, and then he killed. Was he digging around in bodies to find the soul?

The man I interviewed also told me he was under the influence of hypnotic drugs when he killed. I have no evidence that he was ever the subject of a government controlled chemical experiment, but we know now that many people in the armed forces were.

According to respected studies, documentaries, and newspaper articles, several countries began in 1945 to test drugs on soldiers. All the soldiers volunteered, but they were not always told what they were given. Many service people or their surviving family members have since sued to find out what the soldiers were exposed to.

The U.S. Army estimated that at least 1,500 soldiers were given LSD in controlled experiments.

The man I interviewed also told me "authorities make you kill."

That is chilling to speculate about. Did people who were above him in rank when he was in the military actually order him to kill? Of course, we have seen dozens of movies with this very plot, and I have no knowledge of the veracity of his statement.

All the known victims were male. The police officer who worked on this case the longest and a few other investigators have speculated there could be a homosexual element to the butchery.

Some people who have looked at this case also speculate cannibalism could be one answer.

Was he simply a mad man who felt a compulsion to kill and butcher? He was never charged with any murder. If his case had come to trial, we might have some questions answered. But he died in Dayton, OH in 1997 and took his secrets and reasons with him.

# Chapter 3
# A surreal interview with the Mad Butcher

*As a child growing up in Oak Hill, I heard adults talking about a man who was killing people and cutting up their bodies. As you can well imagine, this talk of a Mad Butcher impressed me with fear. As an adult, I researched this man's identify and talked with people who knew him. But the should-be sophisticated reporter found herself reverting to a fearful child for a few minutes when the probable butcher answered the phone. As I found my adult sensibilities return and listened to this mad man, I was amazed to hear him tell me how he views a major division in his world.*

As a child, my ears perked up when one particular neighbor talked to my parents about men who were going missing. This neighbor often ate his lunch at a drug store on Oak Hill's Main Street. Many people gathered there for food and conversation. The drug store was only a few blocks away from the Four Minute Lunch.

When he talked to my parents, this neighbor would include the names of the missing men. I cannot say I have a genuine memory of hearing him say "Ernest Gwinn." But I do remember him talking about how one of the missing men was always dressed up wherever he went. As an adult, when I studied the police file and read about Gwinn, I knew this was the man my neighbor had talked about.

I also had a childish understanding of who Mike Rogers was. Believe me this was terrifying to listen to adults talk about what happened to Rogers and to know he walked the same Main Street I did.

As a reporter for *The Charleston Gazette*, I worked on my notes ahead of time. I knew what I wanted to ask the man I believed to be the Mad Butcher. I even had copies of letters he wrote to some people I knew.

I could have called him from my home, but some inkling made me think I did not want him to somehow obtain my home phone number.

I chose to call him from inside the *Gazette* newsroom. Perhaps I also thought I could take comfort in people being around me. I thought I was well-prepared. But when he picked up the phone, I had to suppress those instinctive childhood fears for a few minutes as I heard his voice.

I had dialed the Dayton Mental Health Center in Ohio. The suspect was a patient there. He was 60 at the time.

I started by asking him about the death of President John Kennedy. From his letters, I knew Kennedy's death affected him.

He told me he was asleep when his cousin called to tell him Kennedy had been shot. He turned on the television to see the events unfold. "I was so shocked," he told me. "I went into mourning for about two weeks. I would not shave or bathe."

He told me he had served in the Air Force starting in 1950 in Brian, Texas and now enjoyed visiting the air museum in Dayton, near his facility.

"The world is divided between those who are sacrifices and those who are executioners," he told me. "If you are born a sacrifice," he explained, "that meant you would be butchered." His father, he told me, was a sacrifice and was butchered.

I was shocked to hear him say how he saw the world divided and how this division in his world worked out.

When I asked him if there was any way to stop the killing, he said, no. "People are blood thirsty."

He also said, "It's international, this thing of being a sacrifice. No one can be warned about it, and no one can prevent it," he said.

He told me he had been in and out of the hospital since 1964, after he killed a doctor. But the doctor I knew to be alive. He repeated this claim several times during our phone call. But the doctor he said he butchered would live many more years and die of natural causes.

He talked freely about men he was forced to cut up before they killed him. Each time he discussed these killings, though, he would say they happened in a Texas hospital morgue. He did, in fact, work in a Texas hospital morgue in the 1950s.

When he described the killings in the morgue, he said, he woke up, found himself naked except for a tag on his toe. He was going to be killed, he said. So, he killed.

The authorities make you kill, he told me. He also said he believes he has killed 10 people.

"The authorities are government people and church people and other higher ups," he said.

Although he told me he has been questioned about killings outside of West Virginia, few facts about these events could be confirmed. He repeated a story about killing two men by throwing them off a train and about killing a man while he was in the Air Force.

An avid letter writer, he laced his letters with quotes from the Bible. In conversations, each time he mentioned someone's name he added the church affiliation for that person. I thought he did that to prove he truly knew each person he mentioned.

He also said the Holy Spirit came over him and then he killed.

He was a prime suspect in the killings and disappearances of seven men in West Virginia. He gave me vivid accounts of four killings in Fayette County in the early 1960s that came to be known as the Mad Butcher case.

He was never arrested for any murder, but he was arrested for destruction of property in 1966 after he took a sledgehammer to the outside of Montgomery General Hospital. He wanted to work as a doctor in the hospital. The administrator knew he had no medical degree, and he was rejected.

He was a member of two prominent families with political connections. His family had him institutionalized before he was ever charged with murder.

He said he has been in and out of the hospital since that time. He also told me he maintained an apartment in Dayton. He is listed in the 1987-88 Dayton phone book. He said he was allowed to go to his apartment on the first and third Tuesday of each month.

The hospital superintendent refused to confirm his statements about his life outside the hospital. She said such privileges are a part of a patient's treatment and cannot be discussed.

The suspect said he could be released again soon. A letter *The Charleston Gazette* obtained written by the suspect's doctor stated that the doctor had been treating him in Dayton for a year and a half. The doctor wrote that the suspect "acted in ways that could be construed as threatening, I have no documentation of (him) ever physically affronting anyone."

The suspect told me that he was afraid to be a sacrifice. "God Almighty is all the protection I need. That's all the help I want." He said God helped him to survive several attacks in the past.

He believes his father was a sacrifice and was butchered by a doctor.

"I was 13-years-old at the time," he told me. "I was just getting old enough to realize what killing meant."

He went on to tell me he tried to prevent the killing, but the authorities voted to kill his father.

He also told me that his father was cut in half and had red-hot irons stuck in him. Then they put his father in a carnival sideshow, he said. Finally, they brought him back to the hospital where his brain was cut out.

He also named two different people as his biological mother and father, not the people listed on his birth certificate.

We talked about the woman he was in love with when he was young. He told me his young love was actually two people. He said at times she tried to fool him with her double.

Several times when he talked about the killings he was forced to commit, he said he was under the influence of "hypnotic drugs."

His voice was strong and friendly. His memory for dates, names, and details clear.

"Are you going to do a story about this?" he asked me. "Yes", I said, "do you think that will help stop the killing?"

"I wouldn't touch this story with a 10-foot pole, if I was a reporter," he told me.

# Chapter 4
# Donald and Theresa Woods

*A teenage girl walked out of Collins Middle School in Oak Hill on an ordinary day to go to her mother's office. She never arrived. For months, her family and police looked for her. Her remains were found, but decades later no one has ever been arrested for her murder.*

As the calendar turned to her 14th birthday, Theresa Woods' parents did not know where she was. But they knew the present she wanted: a color television. She picked it out before she vanished.

After school, Feb. 20, 1986, she started her new routine of walking from Collins Middle School to Main Street in Oak Hill where her mother worked. She got as far as Jones Avenue, but her parents never saw her alive again.

As soon as Donald Woods' former wife Betty called him to say Theresa was missing, he knew something was terribly wrong. He closed his store and started to look for her immediately.

In October 1985, Theresa moved with her mother Betty, and Betty's new husband Rick Holcomb, to Oak Hill. Betty and Rick worked for an ambulance transport service on Main Street.

Theresa became a student at Collins Middle School in Oak Hill, moving away from her father, her grandmother, Delores Keffer, and her former school friends.

Donald Woods told me, "I never thought she was a runaway. I talked to one trooper for over 90 minutes on the phone, trying to convince him she did not run away. She was a scaredy cat."

But to police she fit the profile: a teen whose parents divorced and who had to move away from the life she knew before.

In the clarity of hindsight, Donald Woods told me he knows now that even if the trooper had started looking immediately, they would not have found Theresa alive.

But he believes the wasted time allowed the murderer to cover his tracks. To this day, no one has been arrested for Theresa's kidnapping and murder.

Her maternal grandmother, Bonnie Louise Prather, gave an interview to a reporter for *The Fayette Tribune*. If she had run away, her grandmother wanted her to know she was loved, and she could come home.

Donald Woods knew his daughter was quiet, shy, and afraid of the dark. Her father's home and his mother's home were next door to each other and encircled by the same fence in their yard in Kimberly, a tiny unincorporated community close to Montgomery. But when she had to go between the houses, she always wanted the porch light on. Donald told me she wanted him to stand at the door and watch her go into her grandmother's house.

Theresa Woods disappeared after school in Oak Hill. She was almost 14 at the time.

The last time Theresa visited with

him, Donald Woods sensed something was bothering her. She would not say what was troubling her, but she did tell him she wanted to live with him.

From the first time I met him, I was drawn to Donald Woods' unmistakable sincerity. He truly loved his daughter Theresa. Her disappearance and subsequent murder shattered his life.

He was always willing to talk to me. He wanted to keep his daughter's short life in the public eye.

The day she disappeared, hundreds of students poured out of Collins Middle School. No one saw a student resisting someone trying to force that student into a vehicle. Knowing his daughter so well, Woods has always believed she must have gotten into a vehicle driven by someone she knew.

Woods launched his own campaign to find his daughter. He had flyers printed that showed her in two photos and put the pictures up in stores, post offices, and schools.

In one of life's great ironies, Donald Woods first met Cathy Carroll when he took a flyer to Montgomery City Hall. Cathy, who worked at City Hall, promised to help Donald Woods distribute the flyers. In a few weeks, and in completely different circumstances, Cathy Carroll would be the victim of a torturous murder. Her death will be examined in the next chapter.

Donald Woods offered a monetary reward. He made countless trips to talk with police and politicians. At first, he went to police several times a week. Two years after Theresa's murder, he reduced his police trips to once a week.

In the decades before unlimited calling, he often had a phone bill that was more than $200 per month. He always kept the same phone number. He told me, "If someone has a guilty conscience or if someone saw something, they can still call me."

I think Donald would describe himself as a simple man who just wanted to take care of his family. He became a more sophisticated person who learned how to move through channels of bureaucracy as he searched for answers. He told me, "They promise you the moon, but when you ask for anything—forget it."

A man searching for minnows in Laurel Creek found a skull. John Davis called police June 6, 1986, almost four months after Theresa first disappeared.

Donald Woods told me how hurtful that experience was. "But at least I finally knew where she was," he said.

A Fayette County deputy, Cpl. Everette Steele, one of the people who went on the search, said in all of his years as a deputy he had never before been on the remote logging road. Laurel Creek, near Fayetteville, is a tributary of the New River. Steele also said police "sifted the sand with a strainer."

They found some of her clothing; her blue jeans were still zipped. They also found some of her pretty red hair, her necklace and earrings, one gray boot, and the lavender hooded blouse she was last seen wearing. They also found some bones.

Both state police officers and deputies searched the area twice. They found additional remains each time. All the items were taken to the state Medical Examiner's Office where Theresa's identity was confirmed. The state Medical Examiner declared her death a murder, but he never made her cause of death public.

Donald Woods joined a club no parent wants to become a member of—the parents of dead children club. He became friends with another sad member, Edward Roberts, the father of Cathy Carroll, whom we will discuss in the next chapter.

Donald Woods told me that Edward Roberts took some comfort in their friendship. The fathers truly understood what each was going through.

I also interviewed Donald Woods on the 25th anniversary of his daughter's murder, a horrible milestone to reach. By then, several police officers that worked on the case had died or retired. "New officers do not know the case," Woods said.

"I wonder what she might have done with her life. She wanted to go to college. Would I have grandchildren?" Woods asked.

He went on to tell me that he never imagined life would turn out as it did for him. "Not a day goes by that I don't think about her. I miss her," he told me.

Woods' mother, Theresa's grandmother, died without knowing what happened. "She wanted to live long enough to see someone caught. She used to sit and cry," he told me.

"As long as I have feet and a mouth, I'll keep trying to find out what happened and who did this," he said.

He buried his daughter Theresa Ann Woods with her Cabbage Patch doll in her casket in the Kanawha Valley Memorial Gardens Cemetery in Glasgow.

Like too many of the parents I have written about, Donald Woods died without seeing anyone arrested for his daughter's murder. I think the grief he suffered shortened his life. Donald Eugene "Hank" Woods, Jr., was 62 when he died in 2014.

# Chapter 5
# Cathy Carroll

*The rape of a child and the torturous murder of her mother in their house sent shockwaves through several West Virginia communities. As people learned about what happened, they felt fear. Decades later with no convictions in this case, the fear has turned to frustration.*

About an hour ago, Pam Drennen was a child.

With her friend, they hopped off their school bus. They walked up the hill to their houses with all the normal sounds of children playing in yards and parents welcoming them home. They exchanged a few words about their days, their plans.

A few minutes ago, a bogeyman stepped out of Pam's closet next to her dollhouse, and struck her with a gun. He had a mask on his face and wore a hat and towel around his head to cover his hair. He had on a green Army jacket. He pushed a sock in her mouth and taped it shut.

This minute, she lies dreading the sounds she always found so welcoming before. Her mother will pull into the garage. She will hear her mother's footsteps on the side porch.

How many days she welcomed those sounds!

Now Pam sweats with dread. She has lain on the bed so long that she must relieve herself. Her urine soaks the sheets. She wishes the smell was not coming to her nose, reminding her of how unnatural everything is this moment.

The bogeyman turns on the television, and the sounds from *General Hospital* come to her ears. Then *Scooby Doo* and *The Andy Griffith Show*. How she had enjoyed these shows.

Next up at 5 p.m., *Star Trek*.

Now her dread turns to panic. Tires cut into the gravel. The engine dies.

From the door, her mother calls, "Sissy, I'm home!"

Her heart leaps into her throat. Sweat pours out all over her. The sweat allows the duct tape around her head to pull away. She can see a tiny sliver of her bedroom.

A man's heavy footsteps squeak on the floor.

Her mother cries out in fright. "Gene, why are you doing this?"

"It's not Gene!" Pam dares to call out from her room.

Then she hears a hard blow connect with her mother's head.

"Gene, you don't have to do this!" her mother implores.

A heavy step drags Pam's mother into her bedroom and slams the door shut.

Pam hears the sound of duct tape pulled from its roll. The same sound she heard from the bogeyman's hands as they wrapped her in duct tape.

Her stomach turns as she hears her mother cry out, "Gene, Gene, why are you doing this to me?" The headboard knocks against the wall.

Pam hears the heavy steps come into the kitchen and open what sounds like a bread wrapper. She hears the bogeyman open the kitchen door and throw something out. Her Siberian Husky, Thunder, leaps off the back porch.

The door slams again.

Silence rings in her ears.

"Momma, come help me!" Pam calls.

Silence.

Pam braves running from her bedroom into the bathroom, and she locks the door behind her, the only locking door in the house.

She rummages through the drawers looking for something to cut the screen. Something. Anything! She finds nail clippers. She clips her way through the window screen. Pam prays if the bogeyman hears her that the little slide lock on the door will hold.

Outside the window, the dog looks up at her. No one will bother her if she can get to Thunder.

Pam boosts herself up and out. Thunder is barking wildly. She lands safely, and Thunder shadows her along the fence as she runs as fast as she can manage. Her legs feel strange and wobbly.

She bangs on the door of the house closest to her for help. Please! Please! No one is at home. If her neighbor Penny answered the door, she would not have been as embarrassed as she is now. The bogeyman had pulled her skirt off.

But she must run up the hill to find someone, anyone who can help her mother.

Another neighbor opens the door. Pam explains in words that pump out of her. "Hurry! Help! My mother! A man in the house with a gun!"

Her startled neighbor stares down at the girl who is naked from the waist down. Duct tape clings to her head. The neighbor brings her a blanket to wrap herself in.

Soon police sirens split the air.

Thunder viciously defends his turf inside the chain link fence that defines his world. He holds off three armed officers who want to enter the yard. One officer rams the butt end of a rifle into the Siberian Husky's snarling mouth. But still the dog lunges at the officer.

"Shoot the dog!" Pam yells. "My mom is in there!"

But with a leash, Pam leads the dog away and puts him inside a neighbor's vehicle.

The first officer who entered Cathy Carroll's bedroom that day, April 22, 1986, does not recognize the woman described, "as the most beautiful woman I ever saw." Her face is covered in white powder. A bloody gash mars her forehead. An electrical cord, knotted near her windpipe, is tied around her neck and around the headboard. She is naked.

***

Now Pam is a mother herself. A sudden, unexpected storm rolls into Fayette County knocking out the electricity. In a darkened courtroom, she tells everyone what happened to her and her mother decades ago.

When she goes home that night, she tells her smallest child she is trying to put a bad man away.

## Venus and Mars in her first marriage

"She was lovely," Marshall Drennen recalled of Cathy Carroll. He was the man Cathy married when she was still a teenager.

The high school beauty queen married a tall, handsome Marine. Neither of them had ventured far from Oak Hill but after they married, she joined him on the base in Quantico, Virginia.

While Marshall donned his uniform and worked on the base, Cathy "cooked and cleaned and did what most housewives do," he said. She also continued to study for her high school diploma. They only lived together about a year.

Everyone who knew her thought Cathy Carroll was physically beautiful and had a beautiful spirit.

The young marriage did not last long. When Cathy returned to her parents' home in Oak Hill, she was pregnant with their daughter. Marshall Drennen said his in-laws did not want him to see his daughter Pam. "I did not even have a picture of her," he told me.

But Pam wanted to see him, and on her own initiative, she sought him out. That is how he got to see his daughter, he said.

## Cathy's sister

"I loved my little sister," Connie Roberts Alexander said. She was 9 when Cathy Faye was born. "She was like a little doll," she told me.

The Roberts family lived in Carbondale, and their father worked in the coalmines in Harewood. Both are unincorporated communities not far from Montgomery.

Connie went to Montgomery High School with twin brothers Jackie and Gene Carroll. Gene was the quieter of the two, Connie remembered, and little about him stood out to her. Everyone called Robert Eugene Carroll "Gene."

Connie introduced her sister to Gene, something she always regretted, she told me.

Gene Carroll controlled Cathy's money and movements. He opposed her decision to divorce him. With threats of violence, he kept her and her two children in a constant state of turmoil. Police, court officials, her co-workers, and her family knew she lived in a pressure cooker. Even her divorce lawyer tried not to anger Gene.

Gene Carroll threw sand in the gears of every court option his wife had, trying to delay the divorce if nothing else. He knew a special commissioner was ready to grant her the divorce and order him to pay for her economic support and he resisted at each turn.

A judge found him guilty of contempt for violating his orders. The judge ordered Gene to jail for the violations, but his mother paid his bond and kept him out of jail.

Gene had everything to lose, and he knew it. But he publicly talked about killing Cathy. He told her he had enough money to pay to have her killed. In time, at least two men would testify in court that Gene approached them and asked them to kill her in exchange for $5,000.

Cathy was well liked in her community. Her co-workers said she took time to give attention to senior citizens who came to City Hall for assistance. She had a good reputation as a worker and as a mother.

Her only enemy was her husband. In a just universe she never should have had to fear someone torturing her to death.

## A super stalker

From the time Cathy told Gene Carroll she wanted a divorce he actively made her life a living hell. He claimed everything in her possession was actually his, including the car she drove to work. She parked on the streets of

Montgomery, and he commonly opened her car and looked inside. Many people, including co-workers, saw him do this. He sometimes put chalk around the vehicle to see if the car moved. He even suggested he might wire the car to explode. She would start the car in the morning and not allow her children in the car until she could be sure it was not about to blow up.

Wherever she went, he followed her. Family and co-workers would comment many times on his uncanny ability to show up wherever she went.

He understood what she liked — her China cabinet for example. On his way out of the house once, he picked up a vase and threw it through the cabinet, breaking the glass and some items inside.

In testimony under oath, Gene admitted he threw the vase into the cabinet. He said the vase, like everything else, belonged to him. "I did not need it," he explained. Even one of his lawyers stated in court that Gene did not treat his wife well.

Though he was court-ordered to stay away from the house so not to threaten her, he routinely showed up. He sometimes phoned Cathy from the house to prove to her he could come and go as he saw fit.

Dozens of times, he came to the house at mealtime or bath time and tried to start a fight. Cathy routinely took her children and sought shelter at her sister's to avoid him.

Cathy was a very attractive woman, and Gene was convinced she must have "boyfriends." He stalked these imagined boyfriends. One man was ready to testify in court how Gene Carroll had stalked him in his vehicle and threatened to pull a gun on him. No evidence ever emerged to indicate she was seeing another man.

Gene came to Cathy's workplace, even though he was court-ordered to leave her alone. A police officer had to escort him out of the building. Once he took his fist and hit her hard on top of her head. The pain made her cry out and her co-workers were aware of what he did.

# Thunder, the vicious dog

Inside the chain link fence at their house in Montgomery Heights, Thunder, the vicious dog, patrolled the yard. Gene Carroll said he bought the Siberian Husky for his son.

Thunder had injured many children who were rushed to the hospital to be treated for serious injuries. No one could enter the yard without a family member keeping the dog at bay. Gene Carroll liked knowing that no man would ever enter his castle and take his beautiful princess, thanks to Thunder.

Every armchair detective who looked at this case started with the dog. Thunder had a record, biting at least a half dozen children, and most of them had to be treated at Montgomery General Hospital. Three bite victims filed insurance claims.

Cathy said the dog was registered in Gene Carroll's name, and she wanted him to take the dog away. She wanted to give the dog away, but her husband told her he would take her to court if she did.

Gene Carroll liked the fact that the dog would clearly discourage any men who wanted to date Cathy from entering the yard. In a pre-divorce hearing, Gene said the dog belonged to his son. "We bought the dog for Timmy," Gene said. He also said the dog was not vicious.

Gene's cousin even testified in a pre-divorce hearing, "that dog would eat me up alive if I went inside the yard."

An eight-year-old who was playing in the neighborhood suffered bite wounds to her wrist, hand, arm, and back.

When they were both 13-years-olds, Pam told her friend Heather she would be safe stepping into the yard because Pam was with her. But the dog lunged for her throat and left Heather with multiple injuries. One bite was to the bone. Luckily, Heather's parents were waiting in their vehicle outside the fence. The father was able to pull the dog away.

As an adult, Heather Ballard testified about this experience in circuit court. She told jurors she remembered, "I could see my bone and blood was dripping on my shoes."

One boy who grew up in the neighborhood knew his grandparents warned him to stay away from the dog. Timmy Carroll helped pull the dog off of him, but he required hospital treatment.

Cathy Carroll had to come home from work and put the dog in the house if a utility worker needed to enter the yard. She had to protect her parents from the dog, too.

Pam Drennen testified the dog was inside the fence as usual when she arrived home the day her mother was murdered. "He (the dog) met me at the gate," Pam told police.

While the rape and murder were taking place, the assailant could be confident that no one would interrupt him because the dog would let no one in the yard.

Pam also told police that while she waited in her bedroom, the attacker told her he could not leave because of the dog.

Police found several slices of bread in the yard near the kitchen door and an open bread bag on top of the clothes dryer near the kitchen door. Police have always believed the attacker exited from the kitchen door.

## Five days before the murder

On April 17, 1986, Gene Carroll was inside their house when Pam came home from school. Gene Carroll told Pam she would soon be without a mother. He added that after her mother was dead, she would need to find a new place to live. He also told her it would be his word against hers.

He told Pam that she, too, would be harmed.

At that moment, Cathy was in Montgomery helping her lawyer with his political campaign.

Pam called her Mom to warn her, and Cathy called the Fayette County Sheriff's Department. Two deputies arrived, and Pete Lopez would return after the murder and see the brutality Cathy suffered.

## Who wanted Cathy killed?

Gene Carroll wanted his wife dead. He told a number of people this including Cathy.

He told Cathy he had withdrawn money from their savings account where he worked. He offered to count out $5,000 for her on the dining room table so she could see he had the money to hire a hit man. He also told her he withdrew the money so that she could not get her share of it.

She died hours before they were to be divorced. Gene Carroll made a small amount of money on her death. But most importantly to him, he did not have to pay her any money, which was his goal.

In their investigation, police established that Gene had the opportunity. He told his work supervisor he needed to take two days off because of his scheduled divorce hearing.

Police believed he had both motive and opportunity, but they also believed a second man actually committed the crimes.

Gene Carroll had alibis for how he spent most of the day Cathy was murdered. But police believe he let the attacker in the house and gave them safe passage from Thunder.

As they investigated, police came to believe that Eddie G. Queen actually carried out the crimes.

Police interviewed Charles Keenan who told them Eddie Queen had told him he could earn some money if he was willing to do a hit job. Eddie Queen said a man he knew wanted rid of "his old lady." Queen said the man had $5,000 to pay, but he wanted $1,000 for making the arrangements.

Eddie Queen had financial trouble. Queen's wife had separated from him and moved out of Montgomery. The Queen residence at 601 First Avenue was unoccupied; they were three months behind in their mortgage payments, and still owed $75,000 on the house.

Two and a half months before the murder, this residence caught fire. Inspectors found both gasoline and kerosene had been poured in the living and dining rooms. The liquids trailed to the back door where the fire was ignited. The state Fire Marshall reported that the doors and windows were locked. Without air getting to the combustibles, Montgomery firefighters were able to extinguish the fire before the house burned down. No one was ever charged with this attempted arson.

Eddie Queen was also attracted to Cathy. He met her when he worked at the Montgomery City Pool. His job gave him excuses to call Cathy. Her coworkers said Cathy tried to avoid the calls.

Jean Lorea worked at Montgomery City Hall and told police that Queen was so infatuated with Cathy that he asked Cathy if she would like to get a contract to have her husband killed, turning the tables entirely. This would free her from her marriage and give Queen a chance. Cathy told Lorea that Eddie Queen knew how to get such a contract.

Later, Pam also told police her mother told her that Queen "made her feel spooky."

In his nearly 300-page investigative report, Fayette County Sheriff Bill Laird wrote that Cathy could have rebuffed Queen's advances. Laird wrote that the dehumanizing and torturous way Cathy was murdered could also suggest the killer had "extreme dislike for the victim." Maybe the killer wanted revenge for being rebuffed, Laird wrote.

Neighbors and even police officers saw Gene Carroll and Eddie Queen together in the early hours before the murder. Gene's statement to police acknowledged they were together, but Gene explained that they were moving furniture.

Queen, too, told police they were together during those early hours, that Gene helped him "until either 3 or 3:30 a.m." on the day of the murder.

In the days shortly after the murder, police questioned Queen about his whereabouts. He said he called on two of his insurance clients, but neither were at home. Queen also said he visited with a Catholic priest in Boomer, on W.Va. 61 across the Kanawha River from Montgomery Heights.

Historically, one priest served two churches, one in Boomer and one in Montgomery. Police questioned the priest, Father Eugene Webber, and he remembered that Queen visited him at the Montgomery church. Father Webber also said Queen exited the church through the back door. Both the Montgomery location and the back door would be closer to the Montgomery Heights house.

## Cathy's Last Day

Cathy and Gene Carroll had a son together, Timmy, who was 11 years old when she died. Timmy routinely walked from school to Montgomery City Hall where Cathy worked, and she helped him with his homework.

Five months before the murder, Gene was court ordered not to come to City Hall where police had had to escort him out because of his abusive behavior to his wife. He was also court ordered not to come to her house; police had been to the house because he threatened her. He commonly defied the orders.

He told many people a judge could not order him to stay out of his own house. While he was separated from his wife, he lived with his mother in Charlton Heights, just across the Kanawha River. .

On her last day of work, Cathy talked on the phone with her sister Connie Roberts Alexander. Her sister had witnessed the abuse Cathy endured. Several times Cathy and her two children fled to the Alexander home and stayed overnight. Connie was trying to talk Cathy into staying at her home this night before the final divorce hearing scheduled for 10:15 a.m. April 23, 1986.

In their telephone conversation, Cathy told her sister that Gene had just come to pick up their son, so she hung up the phone.

One of Cathy's co-workers would later say that was the first time Gene Carroll had come into City Hall since he was placed on bond. Cathy told her co-workers it was the first time he had not cursed at her.

On April 22, Gene had had a busy day. He took off from work, and at least a dozen witnesses, some he purposely wanted to see him, saw him driving around in his truck.

Several of his neighbors saw him. One neighbor was taking classes at the former West Virginia Institute of Technology. She left the Montgomery campus and headed home. She saw him in her rearview mirror when she left school at 10:50 a.m. She would later see his truck near his house at about 3 or 3:15 p.m.

A next-door neighbor, Penny Tolley, saw him sometime between 2 and 2:30 p.m. She waved at Gene; he waved back. She also saw his stepdaughter Pam walking toward the house at about 3 p.m.

Several of his neighbors saw him parked at the closed Elkins Market not far from his house. The husband and wife owners of the market each saw him, too. Later in court, police would state that would be 314 feet from the soon-to-be crime scene.

Another neighbor had been fishing at Kanawha Falls. He got back to the neighborhood at 2:45 p.m. and started cleaning his fish in his yard. He saw Gene Carroll's truck headed in the direction of the Carroll house. He also saw Pam walking home from school from the bus stop after he saw Gene's truck go by.

Pam's school bus driver would later tell police she saw a white man running over the bank of the hill near the Carroll residence. She said the man she saw was wearing a blue ball cap and a shiny blue jacket. This man had light brown hair and wore glasses, the driver said.

That same day, Gene parked his truck in Montgomery and flagged down a man he worked with just to talk.

Gene liked to hang out at the Modern Barber Shop, then located at 444 Third Avenue in Montgomery. He was a close friend with its owner, Frank Armstrong. Besides being a well-liked barber, Armstrong drove a school bus. He always started his bus run at 2:15 p.m., so he was never in his barbershop on school days during his bus run.

Gene walked to the barbershop. He called his mother from the barbershop, and she asked him to pick up a package for her at the Sears distribution center located in Montgomery. He did.

Later, he would tell police he was "just killing time."

He went back to the barber shop a second time and asked where his friend was. Gene Carroll affectionately called Armstrong "Run Ball." Of course, Gene knew Armstrong was absent to drive the school bus.

People in the barber shop commented later they thought it was odd that Gene would ask where Armstrong was, clearly knowing he was on his bus run. Gene also asked what time it was. Gene knew the barbershop had a clock on the wall. One of the customers told him to look at the clock in answer to his question.

In his investigative report, Fayette County Sheriff Bill Laird speculated that Gene was trying to create "an alibi within an alibi." Gene clearly made sure that many people saw him on the day of the murder.

Sheriff Laird wrote in his report, "The time period between 2 p.m. to 3 p.m. were times that he indeed could not account for since he was at the crime scene assisting the perpetrator in gaining entry to the crime scene house."

Several people saw Gene across the river on U.S. 60. One person who saw him was the then-mayor of Montgomery, another was a Fayette County Deputy Sheriff. The mayor saw Gene between 3:15 and 3:17 p.m. The deputy saw Gene at about 3:05 p.m.

## What police found

The evidence on Cathy Carroll's body showed that the last moments of her life were pure torture.

With other officers, Fayette County Deputy Pete Lopez returned to the house after being there five days earlier. He was the first to see her body, and later in magistrate's court, he described what he saw. One end of a cord was around Cathy's neck and the other end was tied to her bed. The cord was knotted at her throat.

Her clothes were neatly folded on the bed beside her. Her hands were tied behind her back and duct tape crossed her mouth.

Many years later in Fayette County Circuit Court, the state Medical Examiner gave more details. Dr. Irvin Sopher said white talcum powder "in liberal volume" was sprinkled across her eyes, nostrils, and the bridge of her nose.

He could not explain why. But rhetorically, he asked, "Was it symbolic?"

Dr. Sopher found duct tape on Cathy's face and wrist.

He also found a laceration on her head from "blunt force," which created a "u" shaped laceration. Perhaps the attacker wore a large ring, Sopher said.

Cathy Faye Drennen Carroll was 34 years old when she died April 22, 1986. From two marriages, she was the mother of two children ages 15 and 11. She died from asphyxia after she was strangled by an electrical extension cord tightly wrapped and knotted around her neck.

The attacker raped the 15-year-old daughter Pam in one twin bed in the child's room. After he raped her, he tied her ankles together with duct tape and told her to hop to the other twin bed. He covered her with a blanket.

In her early years of trying to cope with her mother's murder, Pam said, "I used to pretend she was on Amtrak, and she was coming back."

## Money the motivator

At first glance, the unattractive older man who married a young beauty who turned heads could easily show rage at the thought of another man touching his wife. There is certainly evidence to support this theory. Several men testified in criminal court that Gene Carroll accused them of having affairs with his wife, threatened them, and stalked them. He followed Cathy to the grocery store at least once, convinced she "had a boyfriend" who worked there.

But Cathy's father called Gene "money crazy." His desire to keep all the money he believed belonged to him may have been an even stronger motivator for him than thoughts of his wife with another man.

In one divorce hearing, a lawyer asked Gene if he was insanely jealous of Cathy. "No," Gene replied, "Like I said, I would have given her a divorce the first 30 days, if that's what she wanted. If that's what she wanted, I would have given it to her, but she wasn't taking everything from me."

In that same hearing, a lawyer asked him about his "dangerous fits of anger." Gene said, "I deny it. I might tell — if somebody tries to screw me,

I'll let them know about it real quick. I mean real quick."

Routinely, Cathy purchased gas at a Pennzoil Station in Montgomery. Her husband worried she might be having an affair with a man who was also a customer there. The station owner remembered that still another customer, Larry McCommack, was at the station having work done on his car when Gene Carroll arrived.

Larry McCommack joked to Gene that when the divorce was over, Gene would not have the shirt on his back.

Station owner Roy Wiseman heard Gene reply, "She's not going to get my shirt or anything else because I am going to kill her." Wiseman gave this statement to police after the murder.

Gene's first wife was also a strikingly attractive woman, and together they had a daughter.

When they divorced, he was ordered to pay child support. He swore in family court and on the streets he would not pay alimony or child support to a second woman. He even swore he would kill a judge in an effort to stop the judge from ordering him to pay any money to Cathy.

Two men also testified in circuit court that Gene approached them and asked them to kill his wife. He never said, "She's running around on me." He told them both he refused to pay her child support and alimony.

One of the men, Charles Garland Keenan, told police that Eddie Queen approached him and asked him if he would kill Cathy Carroll. Queen explained that Cathy's husband would pay $5,000 for the hit. But Keenan said Queen wanted to keep $1,000 of the fee.

Keenan told police he never planned to kill Cathy, but he strung Queen along. Keenan said Queen approached him several times with this offer.

But Keenan also told police that Gene Carroll approached him directly. A few weeks before the murder, Keenan said he saw Gene near the barbershop where Gene hung out. Gene invited Keenan to get in his truck.

Keenan said, "Gene told me he was going to kill Judge Zane Summerfield. He said, 'I'm going to kill that son-of-a-bitch.'" Keenan added that Gene told him that the judge could not force him to give his wife anything.

She died 15 hours before her divorce hearing, so she was still married to Gene.

Sixteen days after her murder, Gene sought to have himself appointed as the administrator of her estate.

Gene's mother was married to a funeral home operator. Gene had Cathy's body sent to the funeral home owned by his family. Cathy's family had to fight to get her body back and sent to another funeral home.

After Cathy was murdered, Gene clearly pocketed money from their house and a few assets. When police investigated the case, Fayette County Sheriff Laird detailed an accounting of how Gene made money from his wife's murder. Not much, but definitely some money. Perhaps more satisfying to Gene, though, was the fact he never had to pay her another penny.

He defied court order after court order both as they related to coming into Cathy's house and harassing her, and in his refusal to pay her what the judge said she was due. He told Cathy on numerous occasions that she was living in his house, so he could come and go as he pleased — regardless of the judge's order.

He was also court ordered to pay Cathy's lawyer his fees. Gene dribbled out payments of $1 to $5 to Louis Tabit. Even though Gene owed him, Tabit refused to try to collect for fear of stirring up Gene.

In several court hearings, Gene also told the judge and a special divorce commissioner that all the furnishings in the house were his. He finally agreed that Cathy's mother bought the children their bunk beds. But when Pam wanted to collect her bed as she moved out, Gene refused to give it to her.

Pam also wanted a picture of her and her mother. He refused, but he finally relented when Pam agreed to take the picture out of the frame and leave the frame with him.

In his tabulations of how Gene made money from his wife's death, Sheriff Laird makes a compelling case that Gene may have forged his wife's signature on paperwork that paid off the mortgage when she died.

As her husband, he probated her tiny estate and even filed for his losses under the West Virginia Crime Victims Compensation Act three months and six days after Cathy died.

With the house paid off, he sold it for $4,500 more than he paid for it.

He bought himself a 1986 Corvette Stingray.

Gene and Cathy were both listed on the title for the 1982 Chevrolet truck he drove. The judge awarded Cathy use of the 1980 Grand Prix she drove. Gene told the judge on several occasions that he could not award Cathy the use of the car because it was not the judge's car to award.

Cathy gave Gene cash for their mutual expenses like taxes for the car she drove. When the car needed oil, he bought two containers of oil, and she paid him for both.

Gene tried to delay all the divorce hearings. He also argued that he should have custody of Timmy. If he had custody, he would not have to pay child support. He told the court that he had his son more than Cathy did. He also hoped that if he had custody of his son, he would also be awarded the house.

Cathy managed to support herself and the children on the salary she received from the city of Montgomery. After she separated from Gene, she had no checking account. She used money orders to pay her phone bill and paid cash for her local utilities.

After Cathy filed for divorce, officials with Minnesota Mutual Life approved a Mortgage Life Insurance Application for her and Gene on April 30, 1985. The policy was guaranteed to pay off the mortgage in the event of the death of either Gene or Cathy.

The policy was for $11,767.03, one penny shy from what the couple owed on the house.

As Sheriff Laird points out in the narrative he wrote about the case, Gene sought the policy when he was court ordered not to be in the house. Laird also points out that it would be more logical for the couple to seek out this kind of coverage when they first got the mortgage when their marriage did not seem in trouble.

But the insurance application came after they had been in the house more than nine years and during a bitter divorce.

The deed to the house made Gene and Cathy "joint tenants with the right of survivorship and not as tenants in common," Sheriff Laird discovered.

Laird learned that the agent, James M. Styne who lived in Maryland, provided the application through the mail and did not require a notary to witness the signatures.

In August 2004, Sgt. Mike Spradlin of the West Virginia State Police took a copy of Cathy's signature on the application to a state forensic lab. Examiners said the document was of poor quality, and they could not rule out that Cathy could have signed it.

During the divorce hearings, Cathy showed an exact knowledge of all her bills to the penny. She testified that she had a $10,000 life insurance policy through her employer, and she mentioned the bank loan on the house. But she never gave any indication she knew about the Minnesota Mutual Life policy.

When he filed for compensation through the state Crime Victim's Compensation Fund, Gene did not list the $11,228.60 paid from Minnesota Mutual Life to cover the loan for the house.

Gene made no other house payments after his wife was murdered. Minnesota Mutual Life made a full payment on the house 10 days after Gene applied to the Crime Victims Compensation Fund.

In a divorce hearing August 21, 1985, Gene pointed out that the house needed new windows. When he made his application to the Crime Victims Compensation Fund, he also asked that seven storm windows be paid for and that five rooms be painted and four rooms and the hall be carpeted. Officials with the fund rejected this claim.

In his report, Sheriff Laird points out that Gene's stepdaughter Pam escaped the house by cutting the bathroom window screen. This screen "was the only apparent damage to the house that was believed to be associated with this particular crime," Sheriff Laird wrote. "There was no physical evidence at this crime scene indicating a need for the replacement of seven storm windows located throughout the house."

In a divorce hearing, Gene could not answer when asked, "Which of you was providing more than half of the support for (his son) at that time?" Gene responded, "I couldn't answer that. I don't know."

Sheriff Laird contrasted his divorce hearing testimony with his application to the Crime Victims Compensation Fund. While Gene had his lawyer help him apply to the fund, Cathy's father filed an application on his own 10 months and 22 days after his daughter was murdered. The claim investigator awarded Edward E. Roberts nearly $40,000. From that money, Roberts was to be repaid for $1,250 in funeral expenses, and the rest was to be used for the care of his granddaughter, Pam, who now lived with him.

Gene had three of his closest friends designated to appraise his wife's estate. Cathy did not leave a will, and Gene's friends estimated her probate assets at $5,985.89 and the non-probate assets at $40,000.

They listed her half interest in a Chevy truck at $1,000, her clothing at

$1,000, her jewelry at $600 and her furniture at $500. He did not list the 1980 Pontiac.

Gene also did not list the $11,228.60 Minnesota Mutual Life insurance payout in the assets.

During a divorce hearing, Gene had not shared a $469.57 federal income tax check with Cathy. He said at the hearing, "I'll just cash it when I get around to it. No hurry."

He did list the nearly $500 check with the assets he filed in the Fayette County Clerk's office.

"There is indeed some irony," Sheriff Laird wrote, "in the fact that the victim was only able to receive her portion of this refund due her following her death and through the settlement of her estate. By listing this particular check with a receipt date of May 16, 1986 on the final accounting of the estate of Cathy F. Carroll filed on February 26, 1991, it is clear that there was indeed no hurry in providing her with the benefit of her equal portion of this refund during her lifetime."

Gene sold the house Nov. 7, 1988 for $23,000 in cash. This was $4,500 more than the original purchase price of $18,500 he and Cathy paid in 1975. This, of course, is on top of the more than $11,000 that paid the loan off. If he and Cathy had stayed married, or if he had been ordered to make house payments, he would have paid more than $14,000 to pay off their original loan.

Although the few thousand to the good may not be enough to motivate a person to murder, Sheriff Laird speculated that the "cost avoidance" was important to Gene.

## A father speaks

Inside his Oak Hill home with his wife by his side, Edward Roberts told me that the murder of their daughter took the joy out of their lives. They stopped putting up Christmas trees.

The Roberts brought their granddaughter Pam to Oak Hill to live with them, and she started a new school. But her grandfather said she often woke up screaming.

"Every time I talk to one of them (police), they come back with a big lie," Roberts said. He also said he wished that the FBI could have been called in to investigate the case.

## Two men

In addition to Gene Carroll, many people saw a second man in the neighborhood the day of the murder. Eddie G. Queen was a well-known boxing promotor and businessman in Montgomery. He also operated a nightclub in Montgomery called Queen's Palace. Several people who saw Queen also knew his car and could describe the 1978 dove gray Chrysler New Yorker. Queen's wife also had a dance studio in Montgomery.

Queen was always particular about his appearance — an appearance that was described as flamboyant when he stepped into the boxing ring.

But a few witnesses described a man who looked anything but kempt on the evening of the murder.

On the morning of the murder, April 22, 1986, two Montgomery Police officers saw Gene Carroll and Eddie Queen together at approximately 2:30 a.m. in Queen's wife's dance studio. Later questioned about why they were together, the two stated that they were loading furniture on a truck that would be taken to the Cross Lanes area.

When police questioned Gene Carroll about being with Queen, Gene told them he could not remember the exact day he volunteered to help Queen.

When police asked Carroll what he and Queen were talking about in those early morning hours, Carroll told them, "Just general bull."

Nine days after the murder, Gene, with his lawyer present, gave a statement to police. When asked why several of his neighbors saw him driving his truck to his house, Gene said, "I was on my way to feed my dog." Then he added that once on U.S. 60, he realized he forgot the dog food and had to turn around.

Many people talked to police about seeing Queen and his car on the day of the murder. One witness told police she nearly struck a man while driving who was running south in the southbound lane of W.Va. 61. This area was not far from the Carroll house. The driver Pat Underwood said this would have been about 7:45 p.m. April 22, 1986. Underwood had another adult and her granddaughter in the car. Both adults said the man continued to run after they had the close call.

They had no idea who the man was who could have collided with their vehicle. But a woman who worked for Queen's wife saw Queen at about 8 p.m. hurriedly enter the dance studio. Karen Tucker told police that Queen was wearing a T-shirt and his hair was messed up. Normally, Queen always wore dress clothes and made sure he looked neat. She said he was also out of breath.

Queen was aware that many people in the Montgomery area thought he was the killer. He even made a statement denying his involvement to an insurance client of his.

Where was Queen on the day of the murder? He told police that he went to two separate houses in the course of his insurance work, but the clients were not at home. He also said he was visiting a priest in Boomer across the Kanawha River from the crime scene.

In 1986 when Fayette County Deputy Alan Workman interviewed him, Queen never mentioned one alibi witness that he began to rely on starting August 1, 2003. Major General Allen E. Tackett faxed a letter to a state trooper saying he had had lunch with Queen on the day of the murder. Tackett is a well-respected member of the military, and he and Queen became friends because they were both interested in boxing.

At the time, Tackett also worked evening shifts for Hobet Mining. Major General Tacket explained he must have left Queen at approximately 3 p.m. so he (Tackett) would not be late for work. He said he met Queen for lunch at about 1 p.m. But he could not remember if they ate in Marmet or Charleston. The two towns are almost 12 miles apart.

## Interviewing a 15-year-old

What trauma a ninth grade Valley High School student suffered after being attacked and raped, then forced to listen to the sounds of her mother being murdered!

With the clarity of hindsight, several police officers explained that they probably could have been more sensitive in the eight separate interviews they conducted with Pam Drennen.

"I felt tiny," Drennen said of the experience.

After he was assigned to the case, Assistant Fayette County Prosecutor Brian Parsons said police interrogated the child, and they failed to listen to her.

The man who jumped out of her bedroom closet had a stocking over his face, a blue ball cap, and a towel or rag under his cap to cover his hair.

Pam heard her mother call out "Gene, don't," but Pam called to her mother, "It's not Gene."

Physically, Gene Carroll was smaller than the attacker.

In his nearly 300-page report that summarized the investigations, Sheriff Laird wrote Pam Drennen's testimony showed "a remarkable consistency."

Only one person wanted Cathy dead and sought someone to murder her: Gene Carroll. Many people heard him say he wanted her dead, and he promised Cathy that with the $5,000 he laid out on the table in front of her, he had money to hire her killer.

Shortly before the murder, he came to the house to tell Pam that she would need another place to stay and that soon she would not have a mother. He also told Pam that she, too, would be hurt.

After she was taken to an emergency room, Pam Drennen told one police officer to go arrest her stepfather for the crimes immediately. At her mother's funeral, Pam also called out her stepfather.

Pam listened as countless people told her they had seen Gene Carroll in so many locations on the day of the murder. She also learned that while she was trapped in her house with the attacker, Gene Carroll was across the river in his mother's Charlton Heights house playing cards with his mother and Pam's half-brother. Clearly, the only person who wanted the murder had a perfect alibi for his time.

Living in a small community where everyone she knew was discussing the horrific case undoubtedly confounded Pam. But no random rapist and murderer would just happen to be in a child's bedroom before she came home from school. No random criminal could get past Thunder, the notorious attack dog.

Pam knew that her stepfather was in her house when she got home five days before the murder. She listened to him promise her that she would need a new place to live and that she would be hurt.

Countless times, Pam witnessed the threats her stepfather hurled at her mother. She knew he was the only person on the planet who wanted her mother dead.

The original investigators did not make an arrest.

## Almost 20 years later

Almost 20 years after the crime, a new sheriff succeeded in securing indictments from a grand jury. Both Gene Carroll and Eddie Queen were named in those indictments.

When Gene came to Fayette County Circuit Court for his bond hearing, Judge John Hatcher noted that Gene had a "clear and consistent pattern of troubling conduct." The hearing took place in the courtroom of the main courthouse where pictures of the county's judges hang on the walls. One is a picture of Judge J. Zane Summerfield that Gene wanted to kill.

The person who attacked Pam Drennen and killed her mother used duct tape on both of them. Pam told police how her attacker wrapped duct tape around her head so that she could not see him. When she was finally taken to a hospital, emergency room workers cut duct tape off of her.

While she was trapped in her house, Pam told police she could hear the attacker in her mother's room pulling tape from a roll to use on her mother. The state Medical Examiner pointed out that Cathy Carroll still had duct tape on her body when he examined her.

A few years after the murder, Gene Carroll gave Pam what looked like a Christmas gift. The outside of the box was wrapped in Christmas paper. When she unwrapped it, she found a box covered in duct tape. Pam naturally took this like a slap to the face.

Judge Hatcher told Gene that he "exhibits a persistent disposition to resist, resent and disobey court orders and to harass and intimidate people if they fail or refuse to do what he wants them to do."

Several potential witnesses expressed fear that Gene would harm them if he was out on bond. In a 16-page order, Fayette County Circuit Judge John Hatcher wrote in the bond hearing, Gene Carrol did not dispute any of the statements made. The judge then denied the bond request, leaving Gene Carroll in jail.

## Cancer diagnosis

While in the South Central Regional Jail in Kanawha County, doctors discovered Gene had cancer. His lawyer argued he should be let out of jail for treatments.

Prosecutors argued that if Gene was facing both cancer and a murder indictment, he might feel like he had little to lose. Potential witnesses expressed their fear of him.

The judge agreed that the cancer treatment center was closer to the jail than to Gene's residence. Carroll received all of his cancer treatments while in jail.

## Second man arrested

In February of 2005, Fayette County Circuit Judge John Hatcher prepared a pre-trial order for Gene. This 17-page order included the judge's findings of fact on many aspects of the case after Gene was indicted. The judge wrote that his findings "of facts herein found are uncontroverted by the Defendant (Carroll) herein."

The judge also reviewed a statement Charles Garland Keenan gave to police March 30, 1987.

According to the judge's findings of facts, Eddie Queen told Keenan several months before the murder that he (Queen) knew how Keenan could make some money.

Queen told Keenan that he knew a man "willing to pay $5,000 to have his 'old lady' killed."

Based on his review of evidence and testimony, the judge wrote that Queen approached Keenan three or four times with this offer.

The judge also found that Gene Carroll himself talked to Keenan. Gene told Keenan that he planned to kill Judge J. Zane Summerfield himself because the judge ordered him to pay money to his wife.

On Oct. 31, 2006, police arrested Eddie Gene Queen who was 59 at the time and lived in Cross Lanes. They charged him with carrying out the rape and murder.

The two men were to be tried separately.

## At trial

As part of Gene's trial, Judge John Hatcher had deputies arrange a visit to the house where the murder took place. Deputies drove the judge and all the jurors to the small, two-bedroom house.

Every defendant is entitled to see all evidence. Also transported to his former house, Gene Carroll looked around the house with great interest as though he were seeing it for the first time.

As the trial got underway, members of Cathy's family thought that at long last, they might have justice for her. But in December 2006, Judge Hatcher announced "with a heavy heart" he had to declare a mistrial. He said he was unhappy to stop the case, but in fairness, he believed he had no choice. He learned that there was probable misconduct in the witness room. He said it was brought to his attention that one witness was making statements in front of another witness.

In 2007, when the Carroll case came to trial a second time, Brian Parsons, then an assistant Fayette County Prosecutor, told jurors "Carroll promised her (his wife) he would kill her. She was executed by Eddie Queen, and the promise was sealed in the blood of Cathy Carroll. These were prophecies."

Nine people testified they saw Gene Carroll in the Montgomery Heights neighborhood on the day of the murder.

Several of those same witnesses also saw Queen in the neighborhood. One witness, Brent Walker, said he recognized Queen's Chrysler New Yorker because he had worked on the vehicle. Walker also testified that he could recognize Queen himself because Walker remodeled Queen's night club.

Brent Walker saw Queen and Gene at about 2 or 2:30 p.m. on the day of the murder, and they were about 200 feet from the Carroll residence.

Gene's lawyer, Ed Rebrook, told jurors that this was the first time "I've ever had to defend someone who isn't here."

Officially, Rebrook was Gene's lawyer. But as Rebrook saw the case, he had to talk about Eddie Queen.

Rebrook told jurors that Cathy was an "uncommon beauty … a stunning woman and beautiful on the inside, too." He said his client loved her madly. Gene also "became possessive and controlling." Anything that made him worry about Cathy would "set him off like a rocket."

Rebrook said Gene was "a lousy husband." He added that Gene said "stupid things and was a bad husband."

Rebrook told jurors that Eddie Queen fancied himself a lady's man. When Queen first saw Cathy Carroll, he, too, was attracted to her. Queen told people he thought Cathy was "a very, very beautiful girl."

Queen called her at work all the time. Queen even told her, "I'll kill Gene for you."

"That's how much he wanted to get next to Cathy Carroll," Rebrook said.

The defense rested without calling any witnesses. In Judge Hatcher's anteroom where jurors could not hear, Gene said, "I will not take the stand."

When court returned to open session, the judge told the jurors they were not to talk about the defendant's decision not to take the stand. No one accused of a crime has to testify.

The jury found Gene Carroll not guilty. Six years later, at age 70, he died of cancer.

In his obituary, family for Gene Carroll used a picture of him smiling and wearing a billed cap with the letters "WV" on it. They wrote that he was an avid fan of the West Virginia Mountaineers. They also wrote that he loved spending time at the beach and riding one of his two Harley Davidson motorcycles. The family noted that they would hold a future event in May 2014 during Bike Week in Myrtle Beach to spread his ashes. Family members also wrote in Gene's obituary that this final celebration during Bike Week would "commemorate a life lived to the fullest."

Fayette County Prosecutor Carl Harris dismissed charges against Queen without taking the case to trial. Harris said if jurors could not find Gene guilty, he had no faith that another set of jurors would find Queen guilty.

The age of the case always worked against it. One of Queen's lawyers, Lonnie C. Simmons, noted in his motion to dismiss that police first questioned Queen April 25, 1986, three days after the rape and murder. But it was more than 20 years before he was arrested.

Simmons pointed out that police always knew where Queen was during those decades. A delay in the time a crime is committed and an arrest could constitute a violation of Queen's due process rights, Simmons added.

Simmons also wrote that he was "not aware of recently discovered evidence or witnesses justifying this delay."

If Queen's case had come to trial, his lawyers would argue he could not have been inside the house. They would say he was in another community having lunch with former Major General Allen Tackett of the West Virginia National Guard. Tackett was expected to say that they were together until about 3 p.m., the time Pam would have gotten home from school.

Tackett started boxing as a teenager. Former Gov. Jay Rockefeller first appointed Tackett to the state Boxing Commission. Former Gov. Gaston Caperton appointed Tackett as adjutant general of the West Virginia National Guard. He would go on to become the state's longest serving adjutant general.

Queen as a boxer and boxing promoter became friends with Tackett. According to Queen's lawyers, the two were talking about Queen joining the West Virginia Boxing Commission.

As Sheriff Laird wrote in his report, everyone has great respect for Tackett and would not question his honesty.

Why Queen did not tell anyone he was with Tackett on the day of the murder until 2003 was never explained.

Several letters mailed to Queen requesting an interview were never answered.

At the end of his report, Sheriff Laird wrote "Without any reasonable doubt, it is clear Gene Carroll is responsible for the murder of Cathy Carroll, irrespective of whether it was by his hands or those of another."

The first attempt to bring the case against Gene Carroll to trial ended in a mistrial. The second time, jurors found Carroll not guilty. That prompted the county prosecutor to drop the case against the man police believed carried out Gene's wishes.

To this day, no one has been convicted of the murder of 34-year-old Cathy Carroll and the rape of her daughter, Pam Drennan, who was in the ninth grade at the time.

## Chapter 6
# Eddie Brown

*In his tiny world, Eddie Brown stood out for his generosity and kindness. He could also probably win an award for best employee. Everyone knew he carried cash in his pockets. The person who attacked him never thought about the good qualities of the man he was assaulting and robbing. Someone killed and robbed a model citizen. Many people who knew Eddie Brown in the small community where he lived and worked outside of Oak Hill mourned his loss. To this day, no one has been arrested for this senseless murder.*

Someone offered Eddie Brown a woman's blouse to dab his blood, a last act of kindness to a man known for that quality.

Was it a Good Samaritan, now afraid to come forward? Or was it someone with the killer who smashed four holes into Brown's skull?

"Somebody," Eddie's brother Glen told me, "The good guys or the bad guys tried to help him out."

Eddie Brown did not have to work, but everyone knew that six days a week he walked the mile and a half to Via's Sunoco Station along W.Va. 61 in Kincaid, an unincorporated community near Oak Hill. He worked there for 14 years. His boss never required it, but the 72-year-old Eddie Brown always had the station open before 4 a.m.

His brothers, Glen and Howard, and his sister-in-law Carol said Eddie Brown explained he had a few customers who depended on him to be there that early so they could buy gas and get to work.

"But he also wanted the station to be open so the schoolchildren could have a place to go out of the weather. The station was always full of kids. He was like a grandfather to them," his sister-in-law said.

Everyone knew Eddie Brown walked in the dark to the station. They also knew he carried most of his cash in his right-front shirt pocket.

If someone pulled into the station that could not pay for gas, Eddie Brown would pay. Sometimes he was repaid. Sometimes not. It didn't matter to him, his family said.

"If whoever robbed him had only asked for the money, he would have given it to them," his brother Glen told me.

Eddie Brown and his then 67-year-old sister Ola lived in the family home place in Kincaid. He left home about 2:30 a.m. Jan. 22, 1992, carrying his two flashlights. His sister would later tell authorities she heard voices in the dark, but nothing unusual. Neighbors also said the dogs were carrying on.

Dick Marshall and his wife lived in the same community, and they were also out in the dark as they delivered newspapers.

Eddie sometimes walked on the railroad tracks that passed by the Marshall home, and then turned onto W.Va. 61. Both Dick and his wife would give Eddie a ride at times.

"But he wouldn't ride unless it was real cold," Dick Marshall said. "He loved to walk."

After he arrived at the station, Eddie turned off the burglar alarm and tuned on the lights.

Even after receiving what would prove to be fatal head injuries, Eddie managed to walk to the station just like he always did.

"I was looking for him that morning," Dick Marshall said. "Looking into the station, I did not recognize him. His face was covered with blood. When I finally realized it was Eddie, I went inside."

Dick was stunned and said, "Eddie, what's happened to you?"

Eddie Brown was known for his kindness and generosity

Eddie said, "I've got a place on my head that's bleeding." The baseball cap he was wearing was full of blood.

Eddie was walking around in a semi-conscious daze. The Marshalls' saw blood pouring down Eddie's back to his waist. The burglar alarm was still buzzing.

Dick Marshall insisted Eddie go to the hospital and drove him there.

"I didn't know what happened to him until we got to the hospital. The doctor said he thought someone hit Eddie with a pitchfork," Dick said.

Glen Brown said when the doctor showed his family the X-rays of Eddie's head, his brother's skull "looked like a road map" of holes and fractures. One crack circled around to his eye socket and produced a large purple bruise under his right eye and ear that never went away.

Eddie was wearing a hooded sweatshirt, a hooded jacket, and a baseball cap. Family members later told me that they believed the layers of clothing offered some padding for his skull.

Eddie's knees were also injured after the blow to his head knocked him down.

When the Marshalls found him, Eddie was also holding what everyone has always believed to be a crucial piece of evidence. He was dabbing the blood from his head with a woman's blouse.

None of Eddie's family or any friends ever saw the blouse before that day. At first, they wondered if it came to the station as a cleaning rag. But it had no grease on it. It was a brown colored, textured print, and it looked silky.

Who gave Eddie Brown the woman's blouse and why? The force of the blow would seem to indicate a man struck him.

Was a woman with the attacker as an accomplice or a cover? If so, did this woman feel compassion for the injured victim and hand him a blouse to stop the blood? Or did she see him at another place on his path and give him the blouse?

Dick and his wife also said the store did not seem disturbed, except for the dripping blood. That would also seem to indicate Brown was not attacked in the store, the Marshalls said.

Even though he had suffered what would prove to be fatal injuries, Brown was still strong. He was 5-foot-10 and 250 pounds at the time of the attack. In the hospital, he kept saying he had to get up and go to work. Sometimes it would take seven people to put him back in bed.

When he died 29 days after the attack, he had lost 40 pounds.

Police found one of his flashlights not far from the house on his regular path to work. That made family members wonder if the attacker waited in ambush.

Someone took $500 to $600 and a medical card from Eddie's right shirt pocket. At the hospital, his sister-in-law Carol, found $176 in his left shirt pocket. She also found the air gauge he used when checking tires, a pen, and papers in his pockets.

While Eddie Brown was in the hospital, the telephone kept ringing with calls from well-wishers. He got dozens of cards, especially from children who knew him from the gas station. The nurses and orderlies at the hospital liked him. One nurse told his family they still have a picture of Eddie in the hospital locker room.

Although he worked around gas stations most of his life, Eddie never wanted to learn to drive. On the night he died, he took his sister-in-law Carol's arm and told her, "I'm going to ride in a gray Cadillac." Carol asked him if he would be driving it. No, he told her, but he would be in it.

A gray Cadillac hearse carried his body away.

The community mourned Eddie Brown. At his funeral, the minister quoted from some of the cards children sent him. People also wrote letters to newspapers, expressing their sorrow and shock at such a brutal and senseless crime.

The family believes that someone in their close-knit community holds a piece to the puzzle about Eddie's murder. A community group raised $2,000 in reward money for information that could lead to an arrest. The family also circulated reward posters to dozens of businesses.

A pot of coffee once attracted some area men to the small, warm storefront where candy, cigarettes, and newspapers were sold. "The gas station, the post office, and the store are the only bright spots around here to loaf in," A customer and friend, Glen Frazier told me soon after Eddie's murder.

Howard Phillips joined Frazier to talk about their late friend.

"All the neighborhood kids would be here," Frazier said. "Kids that had a hard-up story, he'd give them candy and loan them money."

Phillips said he hoped that someone "gets a case of conscience. Or, if there were two of them, one will get mad and tell on the other."

Former Chief Deputy Everette Steele of the Fayette County Sheriff's Department told me, "Clearly, the motive was robbery. He had no enemies." Steele added that Eddie was well liked in that community.

Dick Marshall said of Eddie that, "He loved life. He loved people. He should still be around. He was in good health."

"This should not have happened to such a beautiful person. We need more people like him in the world," Marshall said.

Twenty-nine days after the attack, Eddie Brown died Feb. 20, 1992. He was buried in the Kincaid Cemetery not far from his family home and not far from where he worked. A memorial for him states that he was much loved in the small community.

In the memorial, he is described as having "a sweet smile, a gentle heart … generous … trusting."

As they mourned him, friends told me that such a kind and gentle soul should have had the kindnesses he gave out flow back to him — not senseless brutality.

Via's Sunoco Station closed years ago and sits empty along W.Va. 61.

No one has ever been arrested for the murder of Dewey Edward "Eddie" Brown.

## Chapter 7
# Rev. Michael Flippoo

*The Right Rev. James Michael Flippo served as a pastor to about a dozen churches in the Church of God denomination. Now he is serving a life sentence in Mount Olive Correctional Complex. From stories I wrote when I was a reporter for* The Charleston Gazette, *court research, and interviews with people who knew him well, I put together this glimpse into his life.*

The Right Reverend James Michael Flippo always had a burning desire. He had a burning desire for a more beautiful house, a better car, a bigger church. He let that burning desire loose.

He burned his cars, his parsonages, and his churches.

He burned one of his homes when his three sons were small. His wife Cheryl and her younger sister who lived with them while she went to college awakened to the sounds and smells of the fire. The two sisters managed to scoop up the sleeping boys. With no help from Rev. Flippo, they escaped the burning house and stood in the snow and ice.

When Flippo burned one of his churches, he always had a list ready of the improvements he wanted in a new church. He met with his faithful followers who immediately set to work on fundraising to build the new church Flippo envisioned.

Speaking of fundraising, Flippo had a special talent for that, too.

The Right Reverend stood behind at least two fundraisers for members of his congregations who were seriously ill. Flippo helped himself to those accounts. He left 24 cents in one, so that he did not have to go through the obvious step of closing the account. That might alert someone to the fact he had stolen the money good-hearted people had donated. They might ask pesky questions.

He could have gone on to a long career of embezzling from his church members and burning his way to glory, had he not been arrested for the brutal beating and death of his devoted wife, Cheryl.

Police found Cheryl Flippo with bits of her broken skull embedded in her brain. At first, they accepted Rev. Flippo's story that a person who had been stalking him for weeks managed to find the couple on a remote path to Cabin 13 at Babcock State Park. Flippo told police he had also been attacked.

His wife's blood and brains had been splattered not far from the bed. Flippo had some scratches on his legs. Apparently, the stalker meant to do a thorough job on Flippo and started with his legs.

The alleged stalker, bent on finding his target, forgot to bring a weapon with him. The stalker had to rely on using a piece of firewood at hand in the cabin.

The stalker put the couple under a strain. Without being seen, the stalker entered their Nitro house and placed a threatening message inside. The message said, "It was seven days to the end." Someone mangled the waterbed where the couple slept.

Mike Flippo told members of the Nitro Police Department he was being stalked.

Members of Flippo's congregation even stayed with the couple to watch over them.

Flippo thought a fun get-away would be just the ticket to get their minds off of this threatening presence.

But, of course, the alleged stalker would recognize the 1991 green, Cadillac Deville Flippo drove. He switched cars with a friend to throw the stalker off the trail. This car was a red Chevrolet Camaro convertible.

On the way to the park, Mike Flippo even played a Beach Boys tape in the car, so the couple could imagine they were taking a happy trip to a safe place. They arrived on Monday night, April 29, 1996.

What could go wrong…? Ahead of their arrival, Flippo made arrangements for the keys. They arrived after the park closed for the day. He specifically asked for Cabin 13, the most secluded cabin in the park, which also did not have a phone.

Cabin 13 was at the end of a row of cabins inside Babcock State Park in Fayette County. The road that ran by the cabins was rough to say the least. Usually, people on mountain bikes or someone driving a maintenance truck for the park were the only ones who used the battered road. Beyond the cabins, the trail became wooded and uninhabited.

## The loss of a devoted wife

Mike Flippo was born in Birmingham, Alabama, Jan. 31, 1948. His family moved to Gary, West Virginia, when his father went to work for U.S. Steel. His future wife Cheryl Jewell was born Jan. 8, 1950 in Gary. They met as neighbors.

Cheryl Jewell Flippo loved her husband from the time they first met as teenagers. They married young. She took her roles as a pastor's helpmate, wife, and mother seriously.

Her siblings who still mourn her said she was the essence of kindness.

Besides always wanting better cars, homes, and churches, Flippo enjoyed spending money. He was never good at keeping track of how much he spent or what bills the five-member family had to pay. The burden of balancing the family finances fell on Cheryl. In frustration, she once cut up Mike's credit cards.

After she was murdered, people appointed to examine the church's finances discovered that Flippo used church funds constantly. Only his name appeared on several accounts, including one dedicated to pay medical bills for a child's organ transplant. He also had many bank accounts around the area where they lived, and he transferred money among them as he needed.

The committee also discovered that items like the paving of the church parking lot everyone believed had long ago been paid in full had not been paid at all.

They examined as much as they could in an effort to patch together the money maze. But in frustration, they had to label one account as a "mystery account."

His parents even contributed money to the church in an effort to plug all the leaks their son created in the funds.

## What police found inside Cabin 13

Early Tuesday morning, in a panic, Mike Flippo called 911 from a payphone. He was so upset, he told the operator, that he could not remember his name. He was barefoot and wearing only a torn and blood-stained pair of white underwear shorts.

A few minutes into the call, though, he told the operator he remembered. "I'm a preacher. I know who I am. I'm a preacher."

A little after 2 a.m., Sergeant Charles Bryant with the Fayette County Sheriff's Department arrived at the park administration building where Rev.

Flippo stood by the payphone. Flippo also told Bryant someone must have stolen his green Cadillac and his car phone. Sergeant Bryant took down the vehicle's identifying information and immediately got on his police radio. He told other officers to be on the lookout for the stolen Cadillac. Maybe whoever stole the car was also the attacker.

With Rev. Flippo in the police cruiser, Bryant proceeded to Cabin 13 where he saw a red convertible parked outside. Flippo told Sergeant Bryant he had no idea who the car belonged to.

It was raining as Bryant approached the cabin. He later reported the ground was very soft. He saw no footprints but his own.

The front porch light was on. As he approached, Sergeant Bryant saw no footprints on the porch. When Bryant stepped inside, he found no footprints or any water on the floor from the rain.

He saw Mrs. Flippo lying between the bed and a wall, her body bloody and battered.

Bryant left the cabin and escorted Rev. Flippo who was walking toward the cabin back to the cruiser. Sergeant Bryant began sealing off the area, welcomed two paramedics who were just arriving, and cautioned them not to disturb the scene. One paramedic came inside to examine Mrs. Flippo, and one paramedic examined Rev. Flippo outside.

Later, an assistant state Medical Examiner would commit to writing the state of Mrs. Flippo's body. She had suffered numerous fractures to her skull so severe that her brain was exposed and the membrane around the skull was ruptured.

Dr. Zia Sabet counted at least seven severe blunt force injuries. One on the left side of her head measured 6 to 8 inches. He also found pieces of her skull bone in her brain.

Mrs. Flippo's cheek was fractured. A portion of her left ear was missing due to the force of the blows she suffered. There was a piece of bark on her cheek from the firewood. He found the pattern of the wood consistent with what he found on her cheek.

He also found bruises on Mrs. Flippo's right and left forearms and fractures to her hands and bruises to the back of her hands that she received while she tried to fight off her attacker. Her eyes and ears bled.

Police found no evidence of forced entry to the cabin that consisted of a small combination bedroom and living area with a fireplace. The cabin also contained a bathroom with a shower, a small kitchenette, and stairs that lead to a small, open loft area.

Fayette County Sheriff's Detective Garland Burke arrived a little after 3 a.m. Tuesday and started to make a list of all he saw in the cabin as he processed the crime scene. Another deputy also took photographs.

Detective Burke found large amounts of blood on the mattress and one pillow. He also found two blue nylon straps near the victim's body and a brown wood-handled long blade butcher knife lying on Mrs. Flippo's right arm. The knife though was not in her arm. Later, the autopsy would show that Mrs. Flippo had no knife wounds.

Near the bed, he saw a split piece of firewood and a round piece of firewood.

He also found a small piece of duct tape near the victim's body. In the cabin's bathroom, he found a roll of duct tape on the windowsill.

Someone soaked up blood from the floor and transferred it to a pillow and the mattress. As he examined the room more closely, Detective Burke believed that someone wanted it to look like Mrs. Flippo died in the bed, not the floor.

Detective Burke saw a rocking chair that had been overturned with fireplace utensils placed under the chair. As he examined the overturned chair, he could find no evidence on the floor of a struggle. He began to think the chair was turned over and the utensils put under it after the victim died.

*Rev. Michael Flippo*

In a pair of gray pants, Burke found Rev. Flippo's brown wallet. Inside the wallet, he found two blank checks on the Landmark Church's account. He found several credit cards and a voter's registration card. One of the credit cards was in the name of one of Flippo's sons.

There was a check written to MasterCard for $351.00. The check was drawn on the Landmark Church's Bank One account. There was also a cashier check from One Valley Bank to the West Virginia Credit Bureau for $590.06. This was also drawn from a church account.

Detective Burke found a note in the left front pocket of the pants with the name Raymond Schuman, which indicated they had a conversation Monday, April 28, 1996. "Account interest bearing account, keep interest for use," Rev. Flippo had written.

At the time, Detective Burke had no idea who Schuman was or what this interest-bearing account was all about. But he would soon.

Burke and photographer, Deputy R.C. Godsey, saw a briefcase on a table near the victim's body. Nothing on the outside of the briefcase gave identification as to whom it belonged. The briefcase was not locked, and inside they found a collection of photographs of the man who would later be identified as Joel Scott Boggess.

In time, Joel Scott Boggess would testify that he and Flippo were on their way back from Lewisburg and talking about baptism. Boggess testified that on April 27, 1996, the two of them turned into Babcock State Park. Boggess had visited Babcock over the years and aways wanted to be baptized there, he said. Flippo baptized him, and the pictures captured the moment.

According to Detective Burke's inventory, the Flippos brought with them to the cabin a Rainbow Study Bible, a green cloth-covered Bible, a book entitled *In Honest Love*, some letters, a pack of cards purchased at Rite Aid, and food. In time, one of Mrs. Flippo's sisters would verify her sister's handwriting in the letters.

Some of the letters were written on stationery decorated with flowers and this verse: "One little flower can gladden the heart As its fragrances and beauty unfold, One little Prayer can brighten life's path With richness of blessings untold."

Another floral page had this verse: "Thank you, God, for quiet places Far from life's crowded ways, Where our hearts find true contentment And our souls fill up with praise."

In a letter, Mike Flippo wrote to his wife, "I have your best interest at heart."

## Victim or suspect?

From the moment he made the call for help, Rev. Flippo was considered a victim. Police listened as he told his version of events.

In the clarity of hindsight, his call for help is revealing. A transcript of the phone call became 30 double-spaced pages of text. The transcript is included in a response to the appeal Flippo filed with the Supreme Court of Appeals of West Virginia.

The first person to answer the Reverend was a Bell Atlantic operator who then connected him to Fayette County's 911 center.

He could not remember his name, he told them. But as they talked, it came to him: Mike Flippo. He had no idea where he was, he told the helpers. But he could see the word "office" on a sign.

The county operator asked him if he could see the gristmill. Yes, he could, he said. That enabled emergency responders locate him.

Rev. Flippo was looking at an object that has been photographed thousands of times. A picture of the Glade Creek Gristmill can be found in gift shops around the world, especially as the mill looks against colorful fall foliage.

The operators kept urging him to stay where he was so that responders could find him.

The Reverend told them, "He hit me with a log."

Whoever hit him also hurt his wife, he said. "Her hair is so beautiful. It has blood in it," he said.

"Please help me, God. I am so scared," he cried into the phone.

"I love her so much."

He told the operators he tried to wake up his wife.

When he could not wake her, "I ran out the door."

After a paramedic took him to Plateau Medical Center in Oak Hill to be examined, he was still considered a victim.

Rev. Flippo said his attacker hit him so hard on the head that he passed out. At the hospital, staff took pictures of him. The medical personnel who examined him described his two head wounds as small. One was on the front of his head and about the size of a half-dollar. One was on the back of his head and about the size of a quarter.

Then they looked at his legs. People in the emergency room began to question his injuries that produced very little blood. But after he examined the Reverend, state Medical Examiner Irvin Sopher was adamant that the leg injuries were self-inflicted.

Rev. Flippo told police that after he and his wife went to bed, he saw a person lying between the bed and the wall wearing a toboggan to cover their face. He also had a rope. Rev. Flippo said he was about to warn his wife when the person hit him in the head with a piece of firewood. This blow knocked him unconscious, he told police.

When he came to, Flippo said he found a man sitting on his lower legs, cutting his legs with a knife. This person who smelled of cigarettes also threatened to cut his penis off.

The next time he came to, Flippo said he felt his wife's hair and found it bloody. He could not wake her, but he said her heart was still beating.

He went for help.

After Flippo was released and returned to his Nitro home, he spoke on the telephone with one of his sisters-in-law. He told her he just spontaneously decided to go to Babcock State Park.

Police soon discovered Flippo made a reservation with a park employee after he and his friend Joel Boggess visited Babcock the first time. He made the reservation and asked for the most remote cabin in the park.

## The photographs

When he examined Rev. Flippo's gray pants, Detective Burke found a customer receipt from Photo One dated April 29, 1996. Rev. Flippo picked up the photos shortly before he came to Babcock State Park. The pictures were of Joel Boggess.

On April 20, 1996, Boggess had been at Babcock, and a park employee asked him to leave. Boggess was driving his red Camaro at a high rate of speed. This was nine days before Rev. and Mrs. Flippo arrived.

The park employee wrote down all of the identifying information for the car. This was the exact same car police found parked in front of Cabin 13. At first, Rev. Flippo told police he drove to the park in his green Cadillac and had no idea who owned the red Camaro. He must have forgotten he traded vehicles with Joel Boggess to throw off the alleged stalker.

Flippo had also been with Joel Boggess as they drove through the park.

Flippo would later explain that Boggess had been considering getting baptized. They decided to perform the rite at Babcock.

They probably did not realize what most visitors to the park know. The park is famous for having some of the coldest water in the state.

## The stalker

Rev. Flippo reported to the Nitro Police Department that he was being stalked. Members of the police force never found credible evidence to support this claim.

Flippo's congregation believed him and took the threats seriously. Each threat seemed aimed at Rev. Flippo, but his wife was murdered.

One of Cheryl Flippo's sisters explained that the stalker first made an appearance eight years before her sister was murdered. The stalker appeared when Rev. Flippo believed he was in trouble, she said.

## The fundraisers

In 1976, Rick McFaddin was a 14-year-old dialysis patient who needed a kidney transplant. He was one of 13 children in his family, living in a small Virginia town.

His older sister attended the church Rev. Flippo pastored in nearby Bluefield, West Virginia. When Flippo and another church member learned that Rick McFaddin needed the transplant, they agreed to help raise money.

Rick McFaddin remembers seeing donation boxes placed everywhere. He also said he knows people wrote checks for the donation.

At one point, the bank account had a healthy balance of $8,000.

"Then my father went to check on it, and there was 24 cents in the account," Rick McFaddin recalled.

His family never confronted Flippo or the other church member.

"When I became an adult, I said someone needs to confront him," Rick McFaddin said.

Years later, the pattern repeated.

If Christy Schuman's grandmother sat down, her hands picked up needles, yarn, felt, anything she could fashion into a small craft item to sell.

If she stood up, she baked something to sell.

She was worried sick about her granddaughter Christy, who needed a liver and pancreas transplant.

In 1995, the family faced the crisis of Christy's health. The family patriarch was an active member of the Landmark Church of God in Nitro. He helped to build the new church after the previous one was destroyed by fire. The former Main Street Church got a new name after it burned.

Everyone rallied around this family. Local beauticians had fundraisers in their salons. Donations poured in.

On Nov. 1, 1995, the child's father, Raymond Schuman, met with Flippo and signed papers to set up the Christy Schuman Fund. Flippo signed the document that was typed in an elaborate script. Raymond Schuman, who still has a copy, thought it looked official.

While Raymond Schuman left the church thinking he had done the right thing for his daughter, Flippo left the church and opened an account in his name only.

At that time, nobody knew that only Flippo's name was on the account.

When he was combing through Cabin 13, Detective Burke found several pieces of paper in Flippo's pants. One note said that Flippo called Raymond Schuman April 28, 1996. The note states it was an "interest-bearing account, keep interest for use."

As soon as word of Mrs. Flippo's murder circulated, Raymond Schuman called the bank. That was the first time he learned that his name was not on the account.

When church officials started looking at the finances for Landmark Church, members wrote, "we discussed the problems with the Schuman fund and listed the checks that were written to withdraw money. We are very concerned about this situation."

The report also asked this question: What was done with the money?

As he played spin the dial with church funds, Flippo could have written checks from the Schuman fund to pay for his other bills.

For example, the church committee wrote that the housing fund for Flippo "was badly overwritten. Mike Flippo's parents made a $10,000 deposit into it specifically for their son which was consequently eaten up by his bad checks."

## The fires

On Nov. 21, 1988, Ernie Hedrick was on the fire truck with other members of the Nitro Fire Department as they rushed to put out a fire at the Main Avenue Church of God.

Hedrick recalled that he saw heavy black smoke coming out of all four sides of the church when they arrived. "It had an awfully good start for that time in the morning," he remembered.

The Nitro Fire Department got the call at about 8 a.m.

In what now appears like a ghostly presence, a newspaper reporter quoted Cheryl Flippo in an article written days after the fire. The reporter quoted Mrs. Flippo as saying her husband was in the church about 30 minutes before the fire broke out.

In that same article, the Rev. Flippo listed the items he always wanted to have in a new church like a larger foyer, accessible restrooms, a sanctuary on the main floor, a stage in the fellowship hall, and a bell.

He told the reporter the building was insured for $240,000.

He also pointed out to the reporter that they already had a rebuilding fund set up with a Nitro bank.

Quick acting Rev. Flippo managed to save a large walnut desk. He was speaking to the reporter from behind the "massive desk," the reporter wrote. Flippo had already gotten the desk, a matching file cabinet, a computer table, bookshelves and a coat rack into a small apartment he rented while he waited for his faithful followers to raise enough money to build his new church. All of those items were in his church office. "My office was the only room that was not really consumed (by fire)," he told the reporter. Every other room of the church was too badly damaged for anything to be salvaged.

As he explained to the reporter, he never had much of an office in any of his other churches. So, two years before the fire, church members built an addition to the Main Avenue Church for his office. He furnished it as he wanted. Luckily, fire spared his choice items.

When interviewed after Rev. Flippo was convicted for murder, fireman Hedrick said he was astonished to learn of all the fires in Flippo's history. He said he and other members of the Nitro Fire Department had their suspicions about the church fire they were called to fight. But he said arson is difficult to prove.

Another fire that threatened Flippo's family: in 1978 in Bluefield, Gina Jewell lived with her sister and her family while she went to college. She and

Cheryl Flippo just managed to rescue the three small boys and escape the fire themselves. Gina said Rev. Flippo was the last to leave the smoke-filled house.

Safely in the car, the six of them drove away. But Gina looked back. "Then flames just shot out of every window. It just exploded," she said.

A few years before that, Gina recalled that Rev. Flippo had a church in Matewan. This fire started in the living room of the parsonage. The living room wall abutted the wall to their oldest child's bedroom.

The Rev. Michael Flippo was a career minister, until convicted of beating his wife to death. He is serving a life sentence at Mount Olive Correctional Complex.

This house, too, burned to the ground.

Add Flippo's parents' mobile home to the list. It, too, burned, and a car Cheryl was driving caught fire.

Another of Cheryl's sisters, Anita Jewell Pratt, remembered that Flippo told the family he wanted a bigger church. "He showed us the lot where he wanted to build. Then after the church burned, they built a bigger church on the lot he wanted," she said.

Each of Cheryl's sisters and brothers said they embraced their brother-in-law as though he were a brother. They believed him and supported him.

After Cheryl was murdered, the siblings say they lost their sister as well as their idea of a family.

Rick Jewell told me in an interview, "We trusted him. I wish we could have saved her."

All of her siblings still mourn this kind person. In hindsight, Rick said,

Mike Flippo was "so accomplished at lying to get what he wanted that no one would be safe."

## The motive

Inside Cabin 13, Deputy Burke found letters that Cheryl and Mike had written to each other. The letters indicate the two were feeling a strain that Cheryl believed was harmful to them as a family. The strain came from Flippo's friendship with Joel Boggess. Boggess worked at a trucking company whose property bordered Flippo's church.

After Boggess started attending Flippo's church, Rev. Flippo put Boggess on a health insurance plan paid for by the church. The Reverend's son was also on the health plan, but his wife Cheryl was not.

In the letters, Rev. Flippo called Boggess a friend, and he was irritated with his wife. "Why can't I have a friend?" he wrote.

Besides his desire to have this friendship, Rev. Flippo chafed at his wife trying to control his finances.

They were awarded $80,000 from a car accident, and she insisted the money be saved in an account that would require two signatures. She knew he would spend the entire amount on anything that caught his fancy.

Even one of his sons would eventually testify in court that their father was a bad money manager. Also in court, Flippo's defense lawyer said Flippo could not manage money.

Rev. Flippo was prayer partners with Tamara Lynn Cremeans, a member of his church and a friend to both Flippo and his wife. Six days before Cheryl was murdered, Rev. Flippo asked Cremeans to pray for Cheryl because she disliked the relationship he had with Boggess.

Rev. Flippo also told his prayer partner that he wanted to buy land with

Boggess. He asked her to pray for God's guidance. Would God think it was a good idea to get a loan and buy land with Boggess?

Flippo and Boggess wanted to buy a 12-acre tract with the idea that they would divide it and sell parts of it.

In March, Flippo took out a life insurance policy for his wife that was set to become effective on April Fool's Day 1996. The policy insured her for $100,000 and made him the beneficiary.

Rev. Flippo wrote the $313 check to the insurance company from the Landmark Church's account. Twenty-eight days later, she was dead at age 46.

Rev. Flippo apparently chafed at the life he lived and constraints his wife put on his spending. Flippo's frustrations powered the blows he landed on his wife's head. As she put her hands up to block the blows, he broke her fingers as he hit away at her.

## The search warrant and indictment

Before a Fayette County Magistrate, May 3, 1996, Fayette County Detective Steve Kessler wrote that Rev. Flippo's story was "without credibility."

Kessler asked for a search warrant that included blood samples and fingerprints from Flippo. After the magistrate granted the warrant, police took Flippo to the state Medical Examiner's office where he was fingerprinted and blood drawn.

In September of the same year, Detective Kessler's name, along with Joel Boggess' name, would appear on the murder indictment brought against Flippo for his wife's murder. According to the indictment, both Kessler and Boggess testified before the grand jury that produced the indictment.

## The trial

The idea that a pastor seemed to have played a lead role in a bad TV movie —*Cabin 13, Please!* captivated audiences.

When the trial got underway at the Fayette County Courthouse, television satellite trucks from stations near and far covered the parking lot.

Inside, every seat was taken in the large courtroom. Cheryl's family occupied the front two rows.

Several men with perfectly coiffed hair attended daily. They were also pastors and members of the Church of God hierarchy. Members of the press had to arrive early. If they got up, they lost their seats.

Many people who did not write for a living also took notes throughout the trial including a Church of God pastor's wife.

Before the trial began, Fayette County Circuit Judge John Hatcher agreed the case could be bifurcated — that means divided into two parts. After the guilty verdict came in, jurors returned the next day to hear the tales of Flippo's embezzlement. The judge believed the jurors should not hear this evidence during the murder trial.

In the first part of his trial, Rev. Flippo was found guilty of murdering his wife. When the jury reconvened for the second part, Oct. 23, 1997, they did not recommend mercy after hearing how Flippo stole money from his church and people in need.

Flippo hired lawyer David Schles who doggedly attacked each piece of evidence the prosecution put forth. He especially grilled Detective Burke.

A member of the West Virginia State Police forensic lab testified that he found a clear, right index finger print inside the roll of duct tape Detective Burke found in the bathroom at the cabin. The print was Rev. Flippo's.

As the trial progressed, courthouse regulars wondered if Flippo would take the stand. Of course, no person ever has to testify in his own defense. But one lawyer wondered. Flippo must have a pleasing voice for delivering sermons, and he must be persuasive.

When the prosecution rested, Schles called only Flippo's sons as character witnesses. Each of the sons said they were only asking the jury for mercy for their father. James Michael Flippo II also testified that they knew their father received a fair trial.

Rev. Flippo had credit cards on him when he went to Babcock that were issued in his son Chad's name. In her frustration with Flippo's inability to take family finances seriously, Cheryl had cut up Rev. Flippo's credit cards. Chad said his father retrieved a credit card in Chad's name from the trash.

Fayette County Prosecutor Paul Blake told jurors that Flippo not only killed his wife, but he killed the relationships he had with all his family members.

Prosecutor Blake also told jurors Flippo showed his wife no mercy as she begged for her life. Her fingers were broken as she put her hands up to ward off his blows that kept coming.

Defendant Schles tried to discredit everything Detective Burke did. After the jury found Flippo guilty, Detective Burke slipped handcuffs on Rev. Flippo.

As part of the explanation of embezzlement, Raymond Schuman of Charleston testified that hundreds of people tried to help his family raise money for his daughter's liver and pancreas operations. They donated $87,000 to the Christy Schuman Fund. From the start, Schuman believed that two signatures were required before any money could be withdrawn from his daughter's fund.

But, after Cheryl Flippo was murdered, Raymond Schuman discovered that only Flippo's signature was on the account. Flippo took almost $16,000 from the account meant to help the child.

When Rev. Flippo's family learned that the money was missing from the child's account, they put the money back. Raymnd Schuman's daughter was able to have her surgeries, and her father told the jurors she was "doing fair" at the time he testified.

Flippo's lawyer did not dispute that Flippo took the money.

After the trial, one faithful member of Flippo's congregation sent the presiding judge a 17-page, single-spaced letter complaining about the lack of defense. The writer expressed his belief that the case was not properly investigated and that Flippo's defense was not properly presented at trial.

The writer wrote of Flippo that, "he had probably cried out all of the tears available in his tear ducts."

The congregation member also told the judge that the real murderer was still on the loose.

The writer admitted that the money stolen from the child's transplant fund disturbed him. But the writer explained "the funds Pastor Flippo removed were primarily used for needs of the church and others."

In the writer's opinion, Schles offered no defense. But most defense lawyers would agree that Schles did his best with what he had. If Rev. Flippo had taken the stand, he would have opened himself to questions from the prosecution.

## Appeals

Some members of Flippo's congregation and his mother never lost faith in him.

Rev. Flippo appealed the circuit court decision both to the Supreme Court of Appeals of West Virginia and all the way to the United States Supreme Court, to no avail.

Lawyers for Rev. Flippo argued that police should never have opened his briefcase or looked at the pictures of Joel Boggess inside the briefcase.

Fayette County Circuit Judge John Hatcher wrote that a nearly hysterical Flippo called for help and police came to the cabin. Police considered all of Cabin 13 a crime scene, including the briefcase that sat on a table a few feet away from the victim's body.

After outlining all the evidence, Judge Hatcher also wrote that if some nameless attacker was brutalizing Flippo's wife, as the medical examiner described, surely this attack would generate enough commotion and screams for help to awaken Flippo who said a blow to his head knocked him out. But Flippo told police he remained unconscious during the horrific attack.

The judge also wrote that if any information from the briefcase was removed from the case, there was still an overwhelming amount of evidence against Flippo.

In an order dated June 2001, Judge Hatcher denied Flippo's request for a new trial.

# In prison

After he went to prison, James Michael Flippo published a book of poems with a lengthy title called *A Collection From Creation: Observations from nature, viewed from the small window of his cell at Mount Olive Correctional Complex, Mount Olive, West Virginia.*

He dedicated the 112-page book to his mother Betty who paid to have the book printed.

The back of the book includes a nice picture of Flippo wearing a jacket and a white tie.

The poem he entitled "Frost" explained that he liked nothing better than licking the spoon and bowl from a chocolate cake that his grandmother made.

He also noted that his wife would save the frosting bowl for him, but "She infrequently made homemade icing for a birthday in our house."

From prison in 2017, Flippo also wrote a letter to the editor that ran in *The Charleston Gazette*. "What is wrong with our country?" the letter began. "Men are paid millions of dollars to play NFL Football and still they can't show any allegiance to the American Flag. I say send them to Iran or North Korea and let them play ball there. I will cease to watch NFL if this disgraceful, racist action continues."

Signed, Michael Flippo, Mount Olive

I have seen no reports of athletes in expensive footwear quaking after Flippo's letter ran.

# Chapter 8
# The Great Unknown

*The English poet John Donne wrote, "Any man's death diminishes me." I agree completely. Each death I have written about always saddens me. The man I am about to introduce you to has a special sadness all of his own.*

Police and prosecutors gathered for a press conference to announce that for the first time the West Virginia police had asked an artist to make a reconstruction of a murder victim's face and head.

"We need a starting point," Sgt. Dale Payne, who worked at the Oak Hill detachment of the state police at the time, explained to everyone at the press conference.

The unidentified man was found April 15, 1994, along Paint Creek, the largest tributary of the Kanawha River. A fisherman found the body. When he was found, he did not match any missing person police knew about.

When the state Medical Examiner studied the body, he discovered that the man had never had any teeth filled or capped. The late Dr. Irvin Sopher was an expert in forensic dentistry. He even wrote a textbook on the subject. When people decided to dig up the body of presidential assassin Lee Harvey Oswald, Dr. Sopher was a crucial member of the investigative team.

After Dr. Sopher examined the man found along Paint Creek, and found he had perfect teeth, which only 2 percent of the population have.

Even though the victim was partially decomposed, police were able to take his fingerprints. Payne said they ran his prints through FBI files, but found nothing.

**WEST VIRGINIA STATE POLICE**
**Criminal Identification Bureau**
**725 Jefferson Road**
**South Charleston, West Virginia 25309-1698**

## UNIDENTIFIED BODY

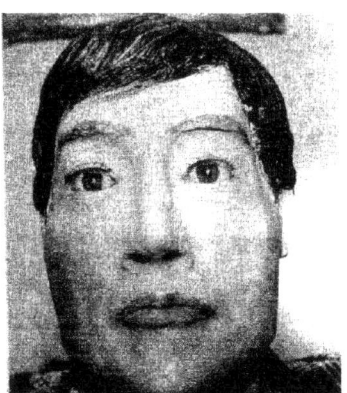
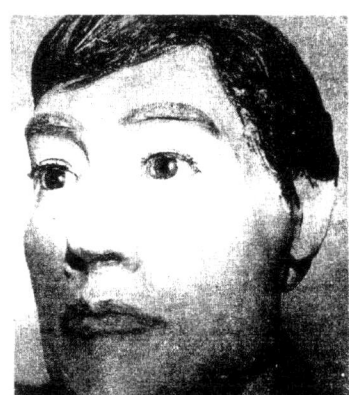

**A partially decomposed body was found on April 15, 1994 along Paint Creek, a stream in a rural area of Fayette County, West Virginia.**

**Subject is a white male, approximately 5' 6" to 5' 7" tall, weight approximately 150 - 160 lbs.**

**Date of death estimated to have been sometime between late October and early November, 1993; and February, 1994.**

**Fingerprints available for comparison, also, teeth can be matched with any available dental records.**

**Anyone with knowledge of this person's identity or having seen this person is urged to contact the West Virginia State Police at 304-469-2915.**

*Artist David Weaver had reconstructed faces for skulls before, with a good success rate. Police asked for his help and added his pictures of the reconstructed face to a poster they distributed.*

Police thought that he died sometime between late October of 1993 to February 1994. Police also believed his death was suspicious.

Police estimated that the white man was 30 to 35 years old, 5 feet, 6 inches tall, and weighed approximately 150 to 160 pounds. After police obtained the reconstructed face and head, they printed up fliers asking anyone who might recognize the artist's version of the face to come forward.

His body was found close enough to a West Virginia Turnpike exit to make police believe that the victim could have been killed elsewhere and simply dumped in Paint Creek.

All these years later, no one has come forward and said this is my son; this is my brother.

State officials told me there are approximately 50 people who remain unidentified at the state Medical Examiner's office.

Whose children are these?

The John Donne poemI began this book with also states, "No man is an island, entire of itself; every man is a piece of the continent, a part of the main. If a clod be washed away by the sea, Europe is the less."

What did we lose with this death of a nameless man?

Donne ends his poem with the now famous line, "Never send to know for whom the bell tolls. It tolls for thee."

Made in the USA
Columbia, SC
11 June 2024